MEDUSA

MEDUSA

IN THE MIRROR OF TIME

DAVID LEEMING

REAKTION BOOKS

For Morgan, Brooklyn and Emilia

Published by Reaktion Books Ltd
33 Great Sutton Street
London EC1V 0DX, UK

www.reaktionbooks.co.uk

First published 2013

Printed and bound in Great Britain by
TJ International, Padstow, Cornwall

British Library Cataloguing in Publication Data
Leeming, David Adams, 1937–
Medusa : in the mirror of time.
1. Medusa (Greek mythology)
I. Title
292.2'13-dc23

ISBN 978 1 78023 095 5

Contents

Preface

Medusa petrifies (*petrificare*, from *petra*, rock). Her face turned the ancients to stone. For Dante she was the erotic power that could destroy men. Freud saw in her hair a nest of terrifying penises signalling castration. For Perseus and his patriarchal culture she was a dangerous female monster to be destroyed. Yet in our time Medusa's reputation has improved. Feminists see her as a noble victim of the patriarchy. The fashion house Versace celebrates the lure of her mysterious face in a logo which stares at us from its ads for men's underwear, haute couture and exotic dinnerware. She is even on the menu of a Disney resort as a Medusa sushi roll. In our mercantile culture she is once again a power player demanding to be recognized. Medusa still transfixes us.

This is a biography, and, like any biography, it is based on an examination of events, descriptions and interpretations recorded by earlier scholars, witnesses and contemporary commentators, and in part on the interpretations of the biographer. In this case our subject's life is described in various – sometimes conflicting – versions by several ancient mythmakers and historians of myth. For interpretations of the events of Medusa's life we can look not only to these mythmakers and historians but to ancient and modern philosophers, modern psychoanalysts, depictions of her in art and literature over the centuries and even to her use by contemporary feminists and the advertising industry. The biographer must, of course, examine the effects of cultural environments and established theories on the recorded stories and their interpreters. Sometimes commentaries reveal more about their authors than their subjects. Furthermore, when the sources for a biography become murky, the biographer can only suggest what, in light of general and specific knowledge of history and cultures, can be supposed to have happened.

What first strikes the biographer of Medusa, whose famous head fell victim to a hero's sickle, is her strangely enduring ability to fascinate (from the Latin *fascinare*, to enchant or bewitch), leading us inevitably to search for a universal reality lurking behind all the stories and interpretations. If many cultures and individuals return in their own ways to the same figure, we can hypothesize that the given figure speaks to the human psyche as a whole. The hero looking for his father or fighting the monster belongs to us all, even though the hero has 'a thousand faces' and wears many different cultural clothes. In short, the biographer of Medusa must interpret her in both her universal and more parochial cultural contexts.

I
The Myth

Earth there produced an awful monster, Gorgon.
Euripides

According to the Greek poet Hesiod, who lived some time between 750 and 650 BCE, Medusa was a direct descendant of the most ancient family of gods. The poet's *Theogonia* (*theogony* meaning 'birth of gods') tells us that Gaia, the original personification of Earth, gave birth parthenogenetically to Pontus, the personification of the sea. Pontus then mated with his mother and produced the father and mother of Medusa: Phorkys, the god whom the great eighth-century BCE Greek poet known as Homer called the 'Old Man of the Sea'; and Keto, the sea monster whose name is related to the word for 'whale' or 'monster'. Phorkys and Keto ruled over the other monsters of the deep. Medusa was not their only child. She was, oddly, the only mortal member of a set of triplets known as the Gorgons. Their other siblings were another set of triplets (Hesiod said there were only two), the Graiae and several monsters. These included Thoosa, the mother of the Cyclops Polyphemos, blinded by Odysseus; Ladon, the dragon-like monster who guarded the apples of the nymphs known as the Hesperides, themselves also said by Apollonius of Rhodes, the third-century BCE author of the *Argonautica*, the story of Jason's quest for the Golden Fleece, to be children of Phorkys and Keto (4.1399); Echidna, a half-woman and half-snake monster; and Skylla, who swallowed sailors, as reported in Homer's *Odyssey*. Of this illustrious but notorious family the Graiae and the Gorgons most concern Medusa.

The Graiae – the Grey Ones, because they were born with grey hair – identified as twins by Hesiod, are definitively defined as triplets in the *Bibliotheca* (*Library*) generally attributed to a second-century

BCE Athenian called Apollodorus. As personifications of the foamy waves, their hair is grey like the rough sea and their names connote the perils of the deep: Deino ('Terror'), Enyo ('Horror') and Persis ('Destruction'). Their sisters, the Gorgons (from *gorgos*, frightening), are described by the author of the fragment known as *The Shield of Herakles*, traditionally attributed to Hesiod, as terrifying beings from whose belts hung snakes, which reared up, stretched their heads forward and flicked their tongues. The Gorgon sisters are named specifically by Hesiod in the *Theogony* as Sthenno, Euryale and, last of all, Medusa, whose 'fate was a sad one, / for she was mortal'. For Homer, in the fifth book of the *Iliad*, she is *the* Gorgon, whose head is 'a thing of fear and horror'.

Other than Medusa herself, the main character in her myth is the hero Perseus. We know that at least as early as the early seventh century BCE the Greeks knew the story of Perseus' decapitation of Medusa, because Hesiod refers to the act in the *Theogony* (270–83). We learn much more about Perseus in the fourth-century BCE writings attributed to the Athenian Palaephatus and especially in the *Bibliotheca* of Apollodorus. The Perseus-Medusa myth is fleshed out in the *Metamorphoses* of the great Roman poet and storyteller Publius Ovidius Naso (43 BCE–17 CE), known in the English-speaking world as Ovid. Ovid probably based his stories on traditional written and oral sources.

It is this myth, told in various parts by storytellers from Homer to Ovid, that has generally been accepted as the definitive myth of Medusa. The myth begins in the Peloponnese city of Argos, said to be the oldest city in Greece. The founder of Argos was Danaus, who came to Greece from Egypt. The inhabitants of Argos were therefore called Argives, Danaids or Danaans, names frequently applied by Homer and others to ancient Greeks in general. Several generations after Danaus, Argos was ruled by Akrisios, who struggled constantly – beginning in his mother's womb – with his twin brother Proetus. Proetus desired his brother's daughter Danaë and he wanted Argos. In a war between the twins, Akrisios won, and Proetus had to be content with ruling nearby Tiryns. Akrisios was told by an oracle that Danaë would give birth to a son who would someday kill him. Falling victim to the delusion that always affects those warned by oracles (the

Danaë and the shower of gold, on a 5th-century BCE krater.

parents of the child Oedipus in the myth of Oedipus the King are prime examples), Akrisios attempted to thwart fate, planning to prevent his daughter from having any contact with men by locking her in an underground chamber. But the gods are not subject to the constructs of humans. Although a more rationalist tradition has it that Danaë was impregnated by Proetus, Zeus himself admits to the parentage of Perseus in Homer's *Iliad* (Book XIV): 'I loved Akrisios' daughter, sweet-stepping Danaë, who bore Perseus to me.' The fifth-century BCE Greek poet Pindar, as well as Apollodorus, Ovid and others, agree that it was Zeus who, in the form of a shower of gold no less, fell with lust upon the imprisoned girl, who in this way conceived Perseus.

So it is that if Medusa's noble ancestry is based in the ancient culture of the earth goddess matriarch Gaia, Perseus' is based in the later but even more prestigious family of the patriarchal sky king, Zeus. The Greeks would have referred to Perseus, like his great-grandson Herakles and several other heroes, as the son of God.

Akrisios, however, refused to believe that his grandson's father was the king of the gods. But whatever the child's parentage, he was not about to keep his future murderer in the palace. Fearing the wrath of the gods if he killed his daughter and grandson outright, Akrisios locked the mother and child in an ark of sorts, which he cast into the sea. The ark washed up on the island of Seriphos, where it was discovered and opened by a fisherman, Diktys, who took the very much alive Danaë and Perseus to his brother, King Polydektes, to raise.

Later, when the king attempted to force a reluctant Danaë to marry him, the king and the now grown-up Perseus became enemies. Polydektes pretended to accept Danaë's refusal and announced that he would marry another woman. He demanded horses as wedding presents, horses being especially valued by all early Indo-Europeans. Perseus rashly promised Medusa's head instead, and Polydektes, knowing full well who Medusa was and the stories of her turning men to stone, immediately accepted the promise of such a gift, assuming that his enemy and the barrier to Danaë's bed would be killed in the process of obtaining it. It should be noted here that the tradition of Medusa's terrifying head having the power to immobilize probably predates Homer. But it was Pindar in his twelfth Pythian ode who first spoke specifically of that immobilization as death by literal petrifaction.

It seems that the goddess Athene (Perseus' sister, since they had a common father in Zeus) overheard the conversation between Perseus and Polydektes about Medusa's head and, hating Medusa for her own reasons, decided to help Perseus on his mission. Athene's feud with Medusa is not made clear until Ovid addresses the issue in the *Metamorphoses*. Hesiod and Apollodorus tell us that Poseidon 'lay with' Medusa, then a young woman of great beauty. Hesiod says they lay in a beautiful meadow on a bed of flowers. But according to Ovid, the union was an act of rape that occurred in a temple of Athene (Minerva for the Roman Ovid), thus polluting a space sacred to that goddess. Athene had no power over her uncle, Poseidon (Neptune), but she directed her ire at the victim of the rape, turning the beautiful Medusa into a figure of horror with a head of snakes rather than hair. But apparently Athene was not satisfied with the extent of

Medusa's transformation and continued to hold a grudge. She therefore accompanied Perseus on his quest, determined that Medusa must be eliminated once and for all. Why a goddess should have had so little sympathy for a young victim of rape is puzzling until we read Apollodorus' offhand remark that Medusa had once 'matched herself' with the goddess in beauty. And we need only read the newspapers today to see that rape victims themselves are often blamed for what happened to them.

According to the mythologist Robert Graves, Athene guided Perseus to Samos, where there were public images of the three Gorgon sisters. She identified Medusa for him and warned him never to look at her face lest he be turned to stone. With this warning in mind, she gave him a highly polished shield in which he could see a reflection of Medusa rather than looking at her directly.

In support of his sister Athene, the god Hermes gave his half-brother Perseus (Perseus and Hermes were both fathered by Zeus) a sickle made of adamantine with which to decapitate Medusa. But his divine relatives told Perseus that he would require more equipment to carry out his mission successfully. He would need a *kibisis*, a container sometimes oddly translated as a 'wallet', in which to place the dangerous head of Medusa; the helmet of their uncle, the underworld god Hades, to make him invisible; and winged sandals to enable him to fly and thus to escape the Gorgons after his killing of Medusa. All this equipment could be found in the care of the Stygian nymphs. But the living place of these nymphs was known only to the Graiae, the triplet sisters of the Gorgons, who lived at the limits of the western world on the edge of night, or, according to some, at the foot of Mount Atlas, and who possessed only one eye and one tooth among them. They passed the eye and the tooth from one to the other as needed. Perseus managed to sneak up close to the Graiae and to snatch the eye and the tooth during one such transfer. The sisters were understandably distraught and begged him to return their precious body parts. Perseus promised to do so if the Graiae would tell him where the nymphs were. The sisters directed him to the land of Hyperborea at the edge of the North Wind. Some say that Perseus now returned the eye and tooth; others say he took them with him.

The nymphs greeted him kindly and provided him with the miraculous objects he sought, and he left for a kind of Underworld at the end of the ocean where the Gorgons lived. Palaephatus says that they lived in the Gorgades, islands in the Atlantic said by some to be the Cape Verde islands. Arriving at the Gorgons' home, wearing winged sandals, the *kibisis* and the helmet of Hades, Perseus discovered the three sisters conveniently sleeping. And what a sight they were. Apollodorus tells us their heads were 'twined about with the scales of dragons' and that they had 'great tusks like swine's', but also 'golden wings'. Others say they had protruding tongues. According to Ovid, they were surrounded by the bodies of men and beasts turned to stone by the sight of Medusa. Carefully, Perseus approached his victim, whose image he had seen in Samos, the only mortal one of the Gorgons. But, not wishing to be turned to stone, he did not look directly at her. He saw only her reflection in the shield given to him by Athene, and with Hermes' sickle he sliced off her head in one blow, his hand guided by Athene. In amazement he watched the winged horse Pegasus and the warrior Chrysaor spring from the Gorgon's body, presumably the results of her having had sexual relations with Poseidon. Pegasus would go on to play a major role in the tale of the hero Bellerophon and the Chimera. Chrysaor would father the three-headed monsters known as the Geryones.

Quickly Perseus placed the head of Medusa in the *kibisis* and began to flee, since the victim's immortal sisters had awakened and were in pursuit. But the magic sandals gave him speed and the helmet invisibility, and he was able to escape.

Ovid tells us that at sunset, after flying a great distance, Perseus arrived at the land of the Titan Atlas. There he introduced himself politely but boldly as the son of Zeus (Jove or Jupiter for Ovid) and requested a place to rest. Such an introduction did not sit well with the Titan, who was no friend of the king of the gods, the Olympians having long ago defeated the Titans in a terrible war in the heavens. He called Perseus a liar and tried to send him on his way. Angered, Perseus took Medusa's head from the *kibisis* and held it up for Atlas to see, thus turning the Titan into an animistic mountain. Atlas' beard and hair became the mountain's forests, his bones its boulders, his arms its ridges and his head its summit. The mountain grew quickly, and from then on held up the sky.

The next morning Perseus flew over the desert of North Africa. According to Apollonius of Rhodes and Ovid, a few drops of Medusa's blood fell onto the desert and turned into fierce Lybian snakes, one of which would later kill an Argonaut, one of the hero Jason's shipmates on the quest for the Golden Fleece.

The flying hero continued on his way over Egypt, and then, as he was passing over the home of King Cepheus and Queen Cassiopeia – usually thought to be Joppa (present-day Jaffa) – he saw a naked young woman tied to a sea cliff. Immediately Perseus flew down to the maiden and fell in love. The girl, he learned, was Andromeda, the daughter of Cepheus and Cassiopeia. Cassiopeia had made the mistake of claiming to be more beautiful than the Nereids, the 50 sea nymphs born to Nereus, the 'Old Man of the Sea' associated with the Mediterranean. Like Phorkys, also called the 'Old Man of the Sea', Nereus was a son of Pontus and Gaia and thus closely related to Medusa, who had herself made the mistake of comparing her beauty to that of a goddess. The Nereids and the sea god Poseidon punished Cassiopeia for her arrogance by sending a flood and a sea monster, named, like Medusa's mother, Keto, to destroy Cepheus' kingdom. When Cepheus consulted the Oracle of Ammon (Zeus Ammon, derived from an Egyptian creator god, Amun) to see if there was something to be done, the oracle replied that the sea monster could be placated only by being given the beautiful Andromeda. The poor girl was chained to the rock for the monster to devour at will. Perseus, however, promised to kill the monster and release Andromeda in return for her hand in marriage. The king and queen agreed, and Perseus killed the monster and freed Andromeda. When Phineus (Agenor), the brother of Cepheus, claimed an earlier betrothal to Andromeda and led a plot against the man he considered a usurper, Perseus held up the head of Medusa for his rival and the other plotters to see, and they were all turned to stone.

Perseus, with Andromeda, now travelled to Seriphos, where the hero discovered that his mother Danaë and her protector Diktys had taken refuge from the now violent king Polydektes in a temple. Perseus went to the palace of the king and announced that he had brought the promised gift. Greeted by insults, he held up the Medusa's head, turning the king and his followers to the circle of stones still found in Seriphos. He installed Diktys on the throne; gave the head of Medusa to Athene, who placed it on her shield; gave the sandals, the helmet of Hades and the *kibisis* to Hermes, to be returned to the Stygian nymphs; and left with his wife and mother for Argos. Ultimately he fulfilled the original prophecy of the oracle there when, in some funeral games, the wind caused his discus to strike and kill his grandfather, Akrisios.

This, then, is what can reasonably be called the canonical myth of Medusa. There are ancient alternate versions of the story. Many of these are attempts to explain away the myth, in keeping with the tendency in some quarters to find historical or at least somewhat rational explanations for the otherwise unbelievable aspects of myths. The earliest such explanation of the Medusa myth is provided in the fourth century BCE by the Athenian Palaephatus, a friend of Aristotle. In his *On Unbelievable Tales* he argues that Medusa's father, Phorkys, was a Cernaean, a native of Cerne, one of three islands just outside the Pillars of Hercules (Herakles), the rock foundations that form the entrance to the Strait of Gibraltar. Phorkys, king of these islands, was said to have ordered the construction of a huge golden statue of the goddess Athene, whom the Cernaeans always referred to, for some unknown reason, as 'Gorgon'. Phorkys died before he could consecrate the statue in the goddess's temple. He left the statue and his three islands to his three daughters, Sthenno, Euryale and Medusa. The three sisters, who remained unmarried, each took possession of one of the three islands and took turns caring for the unconsecrated statue of Athene. The sisters were guided in all matters of state by a kind of guardian or prime minister appointed by their father before his death. Palaephatus calls this man 'the Eye'.

Meanwhile, the Greek warrior Perseus had been exiled from his home in Argos, across the Mediterranean, and was busy raiding cities along the coast. When he heard of the Cernaean island realm ruled by women he decided to attack it. Between two of the islands he came upon the Eye, who was sailing on a mission from one sister to another, and captured him, insisting that the Eye tell him where the treasures of the land were to be found. The Eye revealed that the only treasure of value was the golden statue of Athene, the 'Gorgon'.

When the Eye failed to arrive where he was expected, the three sisters met and began accusing each other of kidnapping him. At this point Perseus attacked, announced his possession of the Eye, and vowed not to return him to the sisters unless they agreed to give him the Gorgon. Sthenno and Euryale agreed but Medusa did not. Perseus then killed Medusa and released the Eye to her sisters.

Perseus now took the statue, broke it into pieces and attached its golden head to the prow of his ship, which he renamed *Gorgon*. (Ironically, many centuries later, a famous French ship named after Medusa would achieve tragic fame, as we shall see.) He sailed around the islands of the Mediterranean and Aegean, killing islanders who refused him treasure and goods. Eventually he made his way to the island of Seriphos and demanded money. The people asked for several days to gather the money, and Perseus agreed and sailed away. But the islanders deceived the invader, setting up a series of man-sized stones in their marketplace and fleeing the island. After that, whenever any islanders refused the tribute demanded by the piratical Perseus he would claim that when the people of Seriphos saw the Gorgon's head they were turned to stone.

Diodorus of Sicily, the first-century BCE author of *The Historical Library*, reported further elements of the pseudo-historical version of the Medusa story. According to him, there was once a war between a race of people known as the Gorgons and the famous women known as Amazons, led by their queen, Merina. Although defeated by Merina, a later generation of the Gorgons became powerful under their leader, Queen Medusa. But the Greek hero Perseus defeated and killed Medusa, and the hero Herakles defeated the Amazons, thus finally ridding the world of realms ruled by women.

In his second-century CE *Description of Greece*, the Lydian Pausanias supports the rationalist explanation, but with variations, in his attempt to explain away the myth. Medusa, he says, was actually a Libyan queen who was defeated in battle by the Greek warrior Perseus. Perseus decapitated her so that he could reveal her great beauty to his fellow Greeks. Eventually Medusa's head was buried in the marketplace of Perseus' home town, Argos.

There are, of course, many other retellings of the Medusa myth. Pindar sang of Perseus who 'raped the head / of the fair-cheeked Medusa'. The first-century CE Roman writer Lucan told in his *Pharsalia* of the Gorgon's serpent hair and described Perseus' flight over Libya and the serpent-producing blood that dripped from his victim's severed head. In the European Middle Ages and Renaissance there are treatments of the myth that can best be approached later as interpretations rather than retellings or explanations of the story.

The rationalist approach provides one sort of explanation of the meaning of the Medusa story but tends to ignore the power of the mythic elements. Myth has a staying power and mysterious depth somehow denied to mere history. The story of Medusa, then, is well known, but the biographer must go beyond the reported 'facts'. Questions remain. Medusa is, after all, a mythical personage who, given her power to fascinate, possibly has a source or meaning that transcends the somewhat absurd and unbelievable events of her myth. Is there a shadow meaning behind Medusa? Is her famous head a mask behind which aspects of human nature hide?

II
Medusa's Lineage

The emblem of the stupefying look.
Tobin Siebers

The first element of the Medusa myth that demands interpretation is her ancestry. The Gaian family of which Medusa was a member is noteworthy for its association with the earth and the sea as opposed to the sky of the Olympians. As depicted by Hesiod and the other Greek mythographers, the Gaians are, quite simply and by definition, monstrous. In their distant past is a war in heaven between their kind and the newly powerful family of Zeus, who had broken away by overpowering and imprisoning in Tartarus his father, the lawless child-eating Cronus. Whereas Medusa's father Pontus, the son of Gaia – earth – the source of all creation, had once been lord of the sea, he became, with the defeat of the Titans by the Olympians, merely the leader of sea monsters under the ultimate kingship of the Olympian god of the sea, Poseidon. Beautiful enough to be an object of Poseidon's lord-of-the-manor lust and to compare herself favourably to Athene, Medusa was punished by that Olympian princess by being turned into a particularly outrageous monster whose story is centred on her terrifying – and eventually severed – head and its ability to turn humans to stone.

Although on the surface Medusa's lineage is clear, there are elements of her persona that lead inevitably to a search for a more universal Medusa lying behind the Greek story. This approach involves first looking for figures that might have served the Greek Medusa as a model, and then considering contemporaneous and later parallel cultural expressions of the Medusa type.

We know from Homer's passing remarks – remarks that seem to assume familiarity – and Hesiod's more detailed ones that Medusa was already familiar to people of the seventh and eighth centuries BCE. In fact, Medusa seems to have been an old story by that time. Given the antiquity of the myth, it is possible that its origins lie outside Greece. We know the myths of the Greek goddess Aphrodite, for instance, but by examining her more closely we discover that she is likely to have been a reincarnation of several more ancient goddesses such as the Sumerian-Babylonian Inanna (Ishtar) and the Canaanite Anat, and when we compare her to Inanna and Anat, a story behind the myths of the three goddesses emerges that unifies them in a shadow being – an archetypal figure who speaks meaningfully to us all. Similar revelations can be revealed when we examine the thematic or archetypal lineage of Zeus, Dionysos and other Olympians.

The centrality of Medusa's head as opposed to her body is a clue to what could be her true origins. In her essay 'The Gorgon Medusa', Judith Suther points out that the Greeks used the Gorgon head as a talismanic mask on clothing, coins, weapons and other objects long before the time of Homer. Homer himself speaks only of her head. In the *Iliad* he describes the presence of 'the head of the grim gigantic Gorgon' on the shield of Athene (5:741); he describes the great Trojan hero Hektor's face in battle as 'wearing the stark eyes of a Gorgon' (8:348); and the shield of Agamemnon on which was 'the blank-eyed face of the Gorgon with her stare of horror' (11:36). The tradition of the *aegis*, the breastplate or shield of Zeus and Athene with the Gorgon's head at the centre, is an ancient one. Homer says that the smithy god Hephaistos made it. In *Ion* the fifth-century BCE playwright Euripides follows the belief that Athene made the shield using the head of the dead Medusa. In the *Odyssey*, Odysseus, when he visits the dead, fears that Persephone will send up 'the gorgon head of some horrible monster'. The story surrounding that head seems to emerge only when Hesiod adds a body and the Perseus elements.

In the search for the Gorgon's origins, the biographer naturally looks to other head-centred myths. To narrow the search we keep in mind the particular characteristics of that head mentioned in the Greek myth. Apollodorus and others claim that the mere sight of her head turned people to stone. Ovid tells us that serpents 'mingled with her hair'. Apollodorus says that her head and those of her sisters

A gargoyle: evil wards off evil.

were 'twined with the scales of dragons' and that her face had tusks. In art she is almost always represented as facing outward rather than in profile. Her tongue protrudes in a manner that suggests pain and death. She is the face of what one Medusa scholar, Tobin Siebers, calls 'the emblem of the stupefying look'.

In ancient Greece a Gorgoneion was an image representing that stupefying look (Gorgon from *gorgo*, terrifying). It was, of course, said to be the look used by Perseus to subdue various enemies and the look carried also by Zeus and Athene on the *aegis*. Gorgoneia were placed on temples and other buildings to frighten away enemies, rather in the same way that gargoyles were used on medieval churches and other public buildings.

In short, the Medusa head was an apotropaic emblem (*apotrope*, a warning). Marjorie Garber and Nancy Vickers in their *Medusa Reader* call it 'terror used to drive out terror', an object with the purpose of 'literally warding off or turning away the evils it embodies'. They suggest that this combination of evil and power for good will serve later students and interpreters of Medusa well as they apply the myth to their own interests, even in popular culture. Later chapters in this biography will support their observation.

An MIT physicist, Stephen Wilk, whose long-time pursuit of Medusa will also be discussed, points out that just as Homer spoke only of the Gorgon's head, the earliest depictions in art of the figure, beginning in the eighth century BCE, consist only of heads. Jane Harrison (1850–1928), the great British anthropologist, feminist and member of the academic group known as the Cambridge Ritualists, wrote in her classic *Prolegomena to the Study of Greek Religion* that Medusa was 'nothing more [than] . . . a mask with a body later appended'. Like other students of early Greek religion, she sees the Medusa head as an aspect of a pre-Olympian religion based on chthonic apotropaic powers and rituals. For Harrison the rituals came first – rituals involving masked figures meant to keep away various forms of evil. Myths such as that of the monster Medusa were developed to 'explain' the rituals, and finally the myth of the monster-slaying hero was developed to account for the monster's

Medusa, Syracuse, Sicily, 7th cenury BCE, clay relief.

Temple pediment featuring Medusa, Corfu, 6th century BCE.

demise. Harrison's interpretation suggests that the Gorgoneia preceded the myth of Medusa and Perseus.

Many of the early Gorgoneia are from Corinth, which is not far from Argos, where Perseus was said to be born. Wilk notes that even when the Gorgon is given a body, as in a seventh-century BCE clay relief from Syracuse and the famous sixth-century BCE pediment figure on the Temple of Artemis in Corfu, the head is large and stylized, almost appearing to have been pasted onto a body.

The Gorgoneia are remarkably similar to each other. They are always depicted facing us with wild eyes and protruding tongues. They almost always have tusks and predominant teeth revealed in a leer. Sometimes snakes are present in the hair. But although the Gorgoneia are often clearly meant to represent the Gorgon Medusa, it should be noted that in its oldest Greek depictions in art the Gorgon is just as likely to be male as female. The faces are often

A Corinthian pot decorated with a Medusa head, *c.* 625 BCE.

A hemidrachm with a Gorgoneion Medusa head, ancient Greek coin, 5th century BCE.

bearded. When associated later more specifically with the Perseus myth, the Gorgon becomes exclusively female and gains a body; later her head becomes not in itself ugly – sometimes, beginning in about the third century BCE, it is even beautiful, as if to emphasize its femininity.

When we search around the world for possible mythical ancestors or other parallel representations of whatever the Gorgon Medusa archetype, or universal symbolic tendency is, we find numerous examples, both male and female. The two oldest examples of such possible Medusa forerunners are the Mesopotamian demon Humbaba of the Gilgamesh epic and the god Bes in Egypt.

The Gilgamesh epic, based on a Sumerian story of the third millennium BCE or earlier, contains an incident in which the hero Gilgamesh and his animal man friend Enkidu enter the sacred cedar forest patrolled by the demon Humbaba (Huwawa). Gilgamesh

A Humbaba head in clay; an ancient Mesopotamian 'gargoyle-Gorgoneion'.

and Humbaba fight and eventually, with the help, according to some versions, of the sun god Shamash, whose power blinds Humbaba's eyes, Gilgamesh and Enkidu succeed in subduing and decapitating their foe. Humbaba, depicted in so-called Humbaba heads of terracotta, is always looking out directly at us with large staring eyes. His face is distorted and his prominent teeth are always bared. Humbaba heads were said to have the power to ward off evil. They have obvious apotropaic parallels with the Gorgoneia of Greece.

The same can be said of Bes in Egypt, whose origins are quite possibly sub-Saharan. If these origins are somewhat vague, we know that Bes was a popular figure in the later part of the New Kingdom, by at least the twelfth century BCE. Like Medusa and Humbaba, he was always depicted face forward, in portrait, rather than in the profile style generally used in Egyptian art. Stephen Wilk reminds us of the archaeologist Eduard Meyer's claim that in ancient art only Medusa, Bes and Humbaba were 'regularly portrayed full face'. Like the Gorgoneia and the Humbaba heads, Bes possessed staring eyes and a terrifying face. His image was often placed in households as an apotropaic symbol to keep away evil.

Many scholars have pointed to possible connections between Medusa, Humbaba and Bes. Clark Hopkins reminds us, for instance, that only the protruding tongue was missing in the Humbaba descriptions and that the Mesopotamian demon was obviously the source for Medusa. Theodor Gaster has also argued for the connection.

The existence of strikingly parallel figures in cultures later than the one that produced Medusa suggests a general human fascination with whatever it is these monstrous figures represent in general. One such figure is the Indian demon Kirtimukha ('Glory Face'). His face is eerily similar to that of the early Medusa, first because of the dominance of his head as opposed to his body. As the story goes, when the demon told the god Shiva he was hungry, Shiva told him to eat himself; Kirtimukha took the god seriously, eating all his own body except his head. That head generates terror with its huge glaring eyes and its horns and is placed as an apotropaic talisman over temple doors and arches. Again, like the Greek Gorgoneia, the presence of Kirtimukha in such locales inevitably

A carving of the god Bes, an ancient Egyptian 'gargoyle-Gorgoneion'.

reminds us of the role of the often grotesque Christian temple guardians, the gargoyles.

Figures in many parts of the world suggest parallels to Medusa. In Indonesia, China and Japan there are monster-demon heads that protect temples or act as ceremonial masks, with their protruding tongues and wild eyes. Some of the most striking parallels are in the Americas. Stephen Wilk identifies several of these. There is the frightening Iroquoian Great Head which is, in fact, a bodiless head with huge staring eyes. Among the Aztecs there are several examples of the Medusa type. The sun god's face in the calendar stone has wild eyes, bared teeth and the famous tongue. Wilk mentions the earth goddess Coatlicue and Xolotl, the evening star, as other examples of the Medusa face. The goddess of death, Mictecacihuatl, with her eyes, teeth and tongue, is perhaps the most obvious example, reminding us also of another terrifying Medusa face, that of the Indian goddess Kali. What all these parallel figures appear to have in common

Mictecacihuatl, Queen of Mictlan, an Aztec goddess of death, 15th century, stone.

A modern Roma Kali, the Indian goddess of change and consort of Shiva.

is the fact that they terrify and that their fearsomeness can be used as an instrument of protection and power. It seems evident that the Medusa of Greek mythology was a cultural expression that emerged from this archetypal family.

III

Medusa in the Middle Ages and Renaissance: *The Femme Fatale*

Should the Gorgon show herself and you behold her
Never again would you return above . . .
Dante

During the European Middle Ages and Renaissance, Medusa became no longer a deformed monster so much as a femme fatale. The femme fatale is one of the most common archetypal obstacles to the successful quest of the universal hero. Like the hero, she takes many forms in the multitude of cultures that have given her form. In the Bible there are several examples. Eve tempted Adam, causing the expulsion from the Garden of Eden. The seductive Philistine Delilah captivated Samson and in so doing undermined the Hebrew cause. The Phoenician beauty Jezebel corrupted the Hebrew king Ahab, turning him to the worship of Baal rather than Yahweh. A 'Jezebel' today is still a 'loose woman'. Another femme fatale, Salome, used her considerable feminine powers to lead King Herod to order the decapitation of John the Baptist. In Graeco-Roman mythology there are several femmes fatales. The beautiful Sirens lure sailors to their deaths. Odysseus avoids this end only by plugging the ears of his crew so that they cannot hear the captivating song of these monsters. He has himself tied to his mast so that he can experience the singing without being drawn to them and killed, as he knew he otherwise would be. We still speak of a 'siren' as a sexually charged woman and a 'siren song' as a relentless call that is impossible to resist. The enchantress Circe turns Odysseus' men into swine and would have done the same to Odysseus himself had he not been saved by the gods. In any case, the hero longing for home did for a while fall under the nymph's erotic spell, thus delaying the achievement of his primary goals, Ithaka and Penelope. Virgil's Dido, queen of Carthage, almost prevented Aeneas, whom she had charmed with looks and sex, from completing the goal of his herohood, the founding of Rome. Later, Cleopatra would be seen by her biographers as a femme fatale, luring the hapless Caesar and Mark Anthony into states of dangerous lethargy. In Arthurian lore Morgan le Fay is a classically dangerous femme fatale, a sorceress who undermines the fellowship of the Round Table. Femmes fatales, perhaps like all beautiful women, are 'enchanting'. In the mythologies of the world, as in countless novels, plays and poems of all eras, beautiful women turn men into de facto stone, immobilizing them, holding them back with their 'charms' so that they can not fulfil their appointed roles in life. One of the most famous femmes fatales in literature is found in John Keats's 'La Belle Dame sans Merci' (1884), a poem in which a traditional hero figure, a 'knight-at-arms', is lured by a beautiful 'faery' woman, whose 'eyes were wild', into her 'elfin grot' to be loved and then deserted. Asleep in the grot, the knight dreams of 'pale warriors, death-pale were they all', fellow victims who cried out to the knight, 'La Belle Dame sans Merci / Hath thee in thrall'. The knight is left bereft, 'alone and palely loitering', his energy and purpose undermined by the femme fatale.

The message of all femme fatale stories is that the woman is powerful because of her erotic charms and that she uses these powers malevolently. Implicit in that message is the idea that *all* women are dangerous and must be kept at bay. This development of Medusa as a femme fatale began early in the Christian era in Greece and Rome and flowered when Christianity attained hegemony in Europe.

The Spanish-Roman poet Lucan in his *Pharsalia* (61–5 CE) concentrates on the association of Medusa with venomous snakes and, in passing, somewhat satirically associates her with Roman women. He suggests that Medusa

> loved to feel the serpents which served for her hair curled close to her neck and dangling down her back, but with their heads raised to form an impressive bang over her forehead – in what has since become the fashionable female style in Rome. And when she used her comb, their poison would flow freely.

In *The Hall*, the second-century Greek writer Lucian asserts that what turned viewers of the Gorgon to stone was not her stare or any magic but rather her extreme beauty: this beauty, which was like that of the Sirens, was 'utterly powerful, reaching to the very essence of the soul; it made its beholders speechless . . . and turned them to stone'. Once again, for Lucian as for Lucan, it was female beauty itself that was dangerous.

Another second-century writer, the Lydian Pausanias, claimed in his *Description of Greece* that Perseus cut off Medusa's head because he admired her beauty and wanted to take the head back to Greece to show it off. To Perseus, according to Pausanias, such beauty, though admirable, was clearly dangerous and thus fair game for decapitation.

The association of women with the archetype of the femme fatale fits well with the gradual tendency of early Christianity to envision women as a threat to the advancement of the male soul. Women are the source of original sin, announced Tertullian (Quintus Septimus Florens Tertullianus, *c.* 160–225), one of the earliest Christian apologists, in his treatise on women's apparel:

> *You* are the devil's gateway: *you* are the unsealer of that (forbidden) tree: *you* are the first deserter of the divine law: *you* are she who persuaded him whom the devil was not valiant enough to attack. *You* destroyed so easily God's image, man. On account of *your* desert – that is, death – even the Son of God had to die. And do you think about adorning yourself over and above your tunics of skins?

St Augustine, bishop of Hippo (354 –430), among the most famous of early Christian commentators, author of the *Confessions* and the *City of God*, said: 'Women should not be enlightened or educated in any way. They should, in fact, be segregated as they are the cause of hideous and involuntary erections in holy men' and 'whether it is in a wife or a mother, it is still Eve the temptress that we must beware of in any woman'.

Fabius Planciades Fulgentius was the writer of *Mythologies*, a series of late fifth-century allegorical interpretations of Greek myths and legends from a Christian perspective. Claiming that the ancient Greek myths needed to be demythologized, his interpretations stress the moral aspects of the tales. Following in the 'realist' tradition of such writers as Palaephatus, Diodorus and Pausanias, Fulgentius, in his version of the Medusa myth, strips it of what he sees as its meaningless elements. Medusa, he suggests, was one of three Gorgon sisters who was particularly cunning and had a head that resembled a snake. Medusa had a power that 'enforces its purpose upon the mind', rather like the way a snake, suddenly met, freezes us in our tracks. According to Fulgentius, the real Medusa, having inherited a great deal of money and land, used her wealth to develop agriculture. Her success attracted the Greek warrior Perseus who coveted her wealth. But rather than marry her or take her as a lover, Perseus killed her and took her land. In this act he was helped by Minerva (Athene). All of this signified for Fulgentius the union of wisdom and masculinity which can defeat the power of the female who would enchant the mind.

The Christian allegorical mode remained popular for several centuries. Bernardus Silvestris, a French philosopher-poet of the twelfth-century, is sometimes credited with having written a commentary on Virgil's *Aeneid.* In that work he takes up the question of Perseus and Medusa, seeing Perseus as the personification of virtue, aided by the wisdom that is Athena and the eloquence that is Hermes, in the process of defeating the evil tendencies represented by Medusa. Another twelfth-century Frenchman, Arnulf of Orléans, approaches the Ovidian version of the story in a similar manner. Perseus, he says, represents virtue assisted by wisdom (Athena) against vice (Medusa). As a woman she represents a sexual threat to men intent on saving their souls.

Giovanni Boccaccio, the fourteenth-century Italian poet best known for the *Decameron,* in his *Genealogy of the Pagan Gods* saw a similar allegorical meaning. For him, Perseus, the son of Jupiter (Zeus), represented prudence and piety in the struggle against vice, represented by Medusa. As Perseus killed Medusa and flew away, so the pious mind thinks of heavenly things rather than of worldly sin. In a sense Perseus, another 'son of God', represents the victory of Christ over his antagonist, Satan.

The fifteenth-century Spanish Jewish writer Judah ben Isaac Abravanel (Leone Ebreo) would see the Perseus-Medusa myth as a similar allegory:

> The angelic nature, which is the child of Jupiter [that is, Perseus], supreme god and creator of all things, destroying and putting from itself all corporeity and earthly materialness, symbolized by the Gorgon, rose to Heaven, forasmuch as it is the intelligences separated from body and matter, which forever move the heavenly spheres.

A sterner account of the power of female beauty is that of Natale Conti in his *Mythologies* of 1551, in which he asserts that Medusa stands for a power that destroys men and must be controlled, as Perseus, 'agent of the divine mind', controlled it with the help of Athene, the representative of 'divine wisdom'.

Such allegories – in which Medusa, a de facto femme fatale, is associated as a woman with the perils of carnality and worldliness in contrast to Perseus, who is reason and moral virtue – are sometimes quite elaborate. In his preface of 1591 to Ariosto's *Orlando Furioso*, John Harrington creates a particularly detailed allegory based on a tradition that held that, after slaying Medusa, Perseus was raised up to Heaven. According to Harrington, Perseus, as the son of God, contained God's heavenly virtue and used that godly power to overpower earthly sin, represented by the Gorgon, and so was carried up to Heaven. Furthermore, for Harrington, Perseus can represent 'the mind of man being gotten by God, and so the childe of God, killing and vanquishing the earthlinesse of this Gorgonicall nature', after which the mind 'ascendeth up to the understanding of heavenly things'.

The evident implication in all these allegorical interpretations is that the primary vice represented by Medusa is sexual temptation. In an anonymous fourteenth-century commentary on Ovid known as *Ovide moralisé*, the author, probably a French Franciscan, goes so far as to refer to Medusa as a '*putain . . . sage et cavilleuse / Decevable et malicieuse*' (whore . . . wise and callous / Deceptive and mischievous). She is '*charnel delice*' (carnal delight), while Perseus represents the deeper knowledge that is Christ.

The association of Medusa with sexuality develops from the views of medieval Christian thinkers on sex and their need to allegorize pagan texts. In the Ovidian version of the story, the one that would have been best known to these thinkers, Medusa is raped by Poseidon, thus presumably establishing her for them as a sexual being. Hesiod and Apollodorus, too had taken note of her pre-monster stage beauty and sexual attractiveness to Poseidon. But none of the classical mythmakers suggests that she was anything other than a monstrously deformed figure when Perseus entered her life. It was not until the story was taken up allegorically in the Middle Ages that Perseus is in any sense threatened morally by Medusa.

The sexual question in connection with Medusa is treated in three major medieval works: the *Roman de la rose*, Dante's *Inferno* and Petrarch's lyric poems dealing with Laura. The *Roman de la rose* in its first incarnation was composed in the early thirteenth century by the French poet Guillaume de Lorris, who died before his work was completed. It was taken up some forty years later by the Paris poet Jean de Meun. Guillaume worked in the context of the prevailing ideals of chivalry, courtly love and courtly poetry. By the time he was writing, chivalry had developed from a warrior code associated with knighthood to a code concerned more with courtly love. Courtly love is a complex ideal in which a tension exists between honour and erotic desire, spiritual growth and sex. A courtier could love his lady – not usually his wife – passionately but through that love could attain spiritual bliss. Courtly poetry such as the *Roman de la rose* – as envisioned by Guillaume – grew out of the ideals of chivalry and courtly love. In short, Guillaume's romance was explicitly intended to express the art of courtly love in all its complexity. It tells the story of the Lover who goes on a quest for a Rose. As is typical of medieval literature and art, the Rose and the Lover are aspects of a complex allegory. In this case the quester represents the art of courtly love and the Rose his lady love. The Lover narrates a dreamlike tale in which he finds his way along a riverbank to a beautiful walled garden and towered castle owned by a nobleman whose name, Déduit, means pleasure in Old French. Helped along and taught the art of courtly love in the garden by the god of love, Eros (Cupid), the Lover meets a series of characters, each of whom represents an aspect of his Rose. Courtesy is there, as are Sir Mirth and Gladness and many others representing attributes. Bad traits are, however, present, too: Pride, Shame and Villainy are examples. When the Lover approaches the Rose, he is chased away by Resistance and is 'reasoned with' by Reason. On a second approach the Lover is helped by Friendship, Candor, Pity and Venus, the goddess of love. Warm Welcome gives the Lover permission to kiss the Rose. But after the kiss the Lover is captured by Jealousy. Here Guillaume's part of the *Roman* ends, having provided what is in effect a psychological commentary on the nature of romantic love.

Medusa does not appear in Guillaume's *Roman*, but the influence of the classical quester's journey into a dreamworld of symbolic importance is evident. Like Jason in search of the Golden Fleece, Odysseus in search of home, Aeneas in search of the new Troy, Rome, or Perseus in search of Medusa, the quester is challenged or helped by allegorical dreamlike figures who represent aspects of human psychology. The Lover of the Rose is helped by the Goddess of Love; Perseus is helped by the Goddess of Wisdom. The Lover is challenged by Resistance; Perseus must overcome the perversity which is the Graiae and the Gorgons themselves.

Jean de Meun's continuation of the *Roman de la rose* is the product of another mind and of an age no longer enamoured of the romantic ideal of courtly love. Meun's approach is satirical and even cynical. If Guillaume was a romantic, Meun is a realist. A primary vehicle for his point of view is Reason. Through Reason and other allegorical characters, Meun satirizes, among many other things, the Church, celibacy and the morality of women. Meun's *Roman* is a gloss on the deceptions and vices of women and the 'art' by which men can have their way with them.

The plot of the new *Roman* finds the Lover still in the garden, still desiring the Rose. He is taught by Reason, advised by Friend and helped by the Goddess of Love. When he approaches the Rose once again he is rejected by Wealth. Chased away, he is rescued by Venus. When Nature confesses to her priest, Genius, she complains that men do not follow her ways. Genius preaches to the troops trying to take the castle and tower, announcing that amnesty and pardon will be given to all who serve Nature via procreation. The fortress is taken;

Venus fires her burning torch into the fortress and the Lover possesses the Rose.

In a common addition to many thirteenth- and fourteenth-century manuscripts of the *Roman de la rose*, the narrator makes a comparison between the head that rests over the Tower of Jealousy, the one into which Venus fires her torch, and the head of Medusa, thus appearing to use Medusa as a comment on the effect of sexual desire on men. This effect is enshrined in the French language, which has a verb, *méduser*, meaning to dumbfound: literally, to strike dumb.

The 'Medusa Interpolation', as it is now commonly called, thanks particularly to the work of the Cambridge medievalist Sylvia Huot, is possibly the work of Meun himself, or more likely an anonymous writer. In 52 lines the narrator of the interpolation reminds the reader of how Medusa turned to stone those who had the misfortune to see her and how Perseus killed her. He then refers to the image over the tower into which Venus fires her torch as an image of greater power than that of the Gorgon. It not only does not turn to stone those who gaze on it, it can also heal, and it can give life back to those who have been *médusé*.

According to Huot, the Medusa Interpolation can lead us to a deeper understanding of how the *Roman* as a whole 'participates in a larger mythographic program . . . exploring the nature of feminine sexuality and its effect on men'. For Huot, the Medusa influence does not begin with the Medusa interpolation but perhaps with an incident in which Guillaume's version of the Lover finds himself at the Perilous Fountain or Mirror that had been the death place of Narcissus. In Ovid's retelling of the Narcissus myth, Narcissus is a beautiful youth more attracted to his own beauty than to the many nymphs and girls who fell in love with him. One of these girls was Echo, so named because when her love was spurned she wasted away to a melancholy whisper. Narcissus, made by the goddess Nemesis to fall in love with himself, died staring at his own reflection in a fountain. In the *Roman de la rose*, Guillaume's narrator sees a marble plaque next to the fountain on which is a description of the boy's death. The marble, then, is what is left of Narcissus. He has, in effect, been turned to stone. For Guillaume self-absorption is one barrier that stands between the Lover and his Rose or between any courtly lover and his lady. As Huot points out, Guillaume's Lover is threatened by a 'despair similar all too similar to that of Narcissus', and is warned by the God of Love that he might be reduced though his approach to love to the immobility of Ovid's Narcissus. Later, in Meun's *Roman*, Reason holds herself up as a better alternative to the petrifying approach of Narcissus; her approach will in fact lead to the Lover's attainment of the Rose.

In the later part of the poem Ovid's story of Pygmalion is related, providing an example of a figure turned from stone to life, from death to fertility in keeping with the beliefs preached by Nature and Venus in Meun's version. According to the myth, the sculptor Pygmalion fell in love with a female statue he had made and prayed to Venus that the statue could be changed from stone to a real woman. Venus answered his prayers and the statue came to life and became Pygmalion's wife. The Medusa redactor uses this story and that of Narcissus to compare the Perilous Fountain of Narcissus with Nature's Fountain of Life, the immobilizing love of Narcissus with the procreative love favoured by Nature, her priest (Genius) and Reason. And, as Huot points out, by juxtaposing Medusa with the story of Pygmalion, 'the anonymous redactor calls attention to the imagery of petrifaction and sterility, while stressing that the Lover has escaped these dangers'. Medusa is associated with sterility – the petrifying quality of Narcissus – while the Lover is associated with Pygmalion and the regenerative power of love.

The temptation is to compare the Lover here with Perseus. Both Perseus and the Lover, as Huot points out, have their 'will' with the 'lady' they pursue. But if Medusa represents the 'dangerous aspect of feminine eros', the Rose becomes for the Lover of the Medusa Interpolation a 'love object that contributes to the perpetuation of life'. Although this is certainly so, it is nevertheless true, as Huot also points out, that 'the dangers of women are a recurring theme throughout the *Roman de la rose*.' In spite of the Medusa Interpolation, the dominant view of women in the *Roman* is that of the femme fatale, the seductive and callous 'monster' who has the destructive power to emasculate and petrify. And Medusa remains the symbol of that power.

In his *Inferno*, the first section of the *Divine Comedy*, written early in the fourteenth century, Dante describes a visionary journey through the Underworld on his way to Purgatory and eventually Paradise. The Inferno is made up of circles in which various sins are punished appropriately. In Circle Five he tells how at the city walls of Dis he and his guide, Virgil, were confronted by the Furies (the Erinyes). These monstrous female figures, who live in the Underworld and have snakes in their hair, stand shrieking and bloody on the tower above the wall. Upon seeing Dante and Virgil they call on Medusa, who could presumably turn the visitors to stone. Virgil, the classical poet who might well have believed in Medusa's power, blocks Dante's vision of the monster, apparently thinking she continues to have power over Christians. At this point an angel appears and drives away the Furies. The poet suggests there is an allegorical meaning 'hidden' in this incident. In his 'Medusa: The Letter and the Spirit', Dante scholar John Freccero discusses that hidden meaning, arguing that just as Perseus had used Athene's shield to block any direct view of Medusa's fatal stare, Dante had to be protected by Virgil from the *erotic* power of the Gorgon, which might otherwise have brought him to the petrification which is unbelief. Once again Medusa is seen from a Christian perspective as a femme fatale – in this case a theological femme fatale – signifying allegorically the powers of heresy and worldliness.

Francesco Petrarca (Petrarch), the great Italian lyric poet of the fourteenth century, most famous for his sonnets, whose name, ironically for the student of Medusa, is derived from the Latin for 'rock', introduced Medusa into his poetry in various ways, always in the guise of the femme fatale. In the most obvious application, the poet describes in his sonnets the immobilizing power of Laura, the unattainable object of his desires: 'the blond locks and the curling snare that so softly bind tight my / soul . . .'.

It is not absolutely clear that there was a Laura. It has been suggested by many that she was a fiction created by Petrarch for poetic purposes. Dante's *Rime Petrose* of 1296 – based on the idea of the power of a stone-hearted beloved named, appropriately, Petra – has a clear influence on Laura's Medusa-like powers. Dante complains of a cruel lady whose heartlessness, like the gaze of Medusa, might turn him to stone. Perhaps more importantly, he raises the idea of the aesthetic problem of self-absorption of the poet in his own creation. By idolizing his 'lady', as it were, the poet immobilizes himself.

Whether a real person or not, Laura was central to Petrarch's aesthetic, and it is this aesthetic aspect that most clearly involves the Medusa figure in Petrarch's work. The idea of the Narcissus-like petrified lover plays a central role in the *Rime sparse* (the sonnets and other lyrics). As Laura's eyes have the power to turn Petrarch the poet to marble, as she gazes at him in his poetry, the poet is immobilized, becoming, like Narcissus, the victim of his self-projection through the creation of an idol. In his *Canzoniere*, Petrarch the poet, like Ovid's Pygmalion, falls in love with his own creation and is in turn re-created and petrified by her, becoming his own representation. Laura has become a Medusa rather than a beloved. In Number 179 of his *Rime sparse* Petrarch writes: 'Medusa and my error [Laura?] have made me a stone dripping vain mixture' – in short, a re-embodiment of Narcissus. Medusa as femme fatale works in many ways.

The theme of Medusa as femme fatale continues well into the Renaissance and beyond, especially in painting. In the well-known seventeenth-century work attributed to Peter Paul Rubens, for instance, the snakes and scorpions that surround Medusa's head suggest an extreme version of the type, the poisonous creatures representing the venomous power of women. Susan Koslow suggests that

> Perseus' decapitation of Medusa may well be read as a sign of retribution and as an assertion of male dominion. When Perseus beheads Medusa he not only vanquishes her, but gains control over her deadly weaponry. Yet, though now commanding it, Perseus cannot contain the creatures Medusa's corrupted body generates. They proliferate unchecked, disseminating evil throughout the world. They are a reminder that the capacity to engender evil is not unique to Medusa but inherent in all women.

Easily the best-known depiction of Medusa is the *Head of Medusa* (1597) by Caravaggio, perhaps influenced by a now lost painting by Leonardo da Vinci. Here the femme fatale, blood streaming from her neck, is depicted still living at the precise moment of decapitation. This is the horrifying nightmare of decapitation – ultimate self-realization. The eyes are angry, as are the snakes in her hair; the

Peter Paul Rubens, *The Severed Head of Medusa*, 1617, oil on canvas.

mouth of what is by no means an ugly face, if a slightly masculine one (Caravaggio used a boy as his model for the painting), is open in a scream of unbelief and surprise. The painting is not an apotropaic talisman; it is a celebration of the destruction of a beautiful but dangerous power.

In summary, the use of Medusa as a femme fatale, whose temptations of the male warranted destruction or repression, coincided perfectly with medieval and Renaissance Christianity's wariness and mistrust before what was seen as the erotic power of women. For the collective psyche of this period, then, Medusa is not relegated to the ends of the earth, where she waited to be destroyed by the masculine hero, as she was in the case of classical thought. She is, rather, a potentially monstrous presence that is always among us. Mother, sister, daughter, wife: all are potentially Medusa. And it must be said that Christianity is not alone as a religious system that sees in womankind the image of the femme fatale. Judaism, Islam and the great religions of India and the Far East, dominated by patriarchal attitudes, have traditionally 'protected' women by way of clothing, social status and religious, familial and political leadership restrictions. In many cases these restrictions are justified by religions pointing to the effect that women have on men – that is to say, the sexual effect. In the Graeco-Roman myth Perseus decapitates the monster and uses her head to advance good causes, good at least from his and his

Caravaggio, *Medusa*, *c.* 1596, oil on canvas mounted on wood.

culture's perspective. He uses Medusa's power to defeat enemies of Olympian order. Although Britomart, the female knight and champion of chastity in Edmund Spenser's *The Faerie Queene*, like Athene, carries a 'Gorgonian shield', and in John Milton's *Comus* a similar shield is referred to as 'the arms of chastity', and 'Medusa with Gorgonian terror' obstructs the path to relief from the pains of Hell in *Paradise Lost*, this side of the Medusa myth seems to be mostly absent from the medieval and Renaissance view of Medusa as the femme fatale. Medusa in this period loses her Gorgoneion status. The apotropaic severed head is a rarity.

Medusa in the original myth as it developed from Homer to Ovid was a sexual being only peripherally; she had once long ago been attractive enough to capture the attention of Poseidon. But, at least according to the Ovidian tradition, she had not enticed Poseidon but had been raped by him. Once Athene had dealt with her out of jealousy or anger, Medusa became physically a monster, a female no longer sexual, a being relegated to oblivion, until Perseus killed her and put her head to good use. In the medieval and Renaissance view Medusa is only monstrous *because* she is beautiful, and feminine beauty is the natural enemy of the quest of the male soul for union with the deity.

IV

Medusa in the Romantic and Victorian Ages: *The Beautiful Victim*

The tempestuous loveliness of terror.
Percy Bysshe Shelley

It was Pindar, in his twelfth Pythian ode of around 490 BCE, who gave the first hint of what for the Romantic Age and many Victorians would become sympathy for a beautiful victim when he referred to the 'lovely-cheeked Medusa's head' chopped off by Perseus. The element of beauty had already been emphasized by those in previous ages who had seen Medusa as a femme fatale. With the advent of Romanticism, sexuality and female beauty became a source of positive ecstasy. Sex and beauty could stimulate the emotions, and emotions were preferable to classical restraint. Furthermore, it was the Romantics' admiration for resistance to power, including that of the religious establishment – as well as their fascination with the exotic and the sensual, with emotional and physical extremes, and with death – that led to their seeing the Gorgon primarily as a victim rather than as a dangerous monster that needed to be destroyed.

In the Romantic interpretation of the story Perseus represents the status quo and the unbending rules of the previous ages, while Medusa is the beautiful exotic victim, perhaps a representation of the persecuted artist longing to be free of those rules. Mario Praz in his classic work *The Romantic Agony* claims that 'this glassy-eyed, severed female head, this horrible, fascinating Medusa, was to be the object of the dark loves of the Romantics and the Decadents throughout the whole of the [nineteenth] century.'

The title of Praz's first chapter is 'The Beauty of the Medusa'. Here he sees the beauty represented by Medusa's severed head as 'almost a manifesto of the conception of Beauty peculiar to the Romantics'. This is a beauty based in combinations of pleasure and

The Medusa Rondanini, probably a Roman copy of a 5th-century BCE Greek statue head.

pain, beauty and death. Praz points to such works as Anna Laetitia Aikin's 'An Inquiry into those Kinds of Distress which Excite Agreeable Sensations', Nathan Drake's 'On Objects of Terror' and William Collins's 'Ode to Fear'. These lines from Collins's 'Ode' provide a good example:

> O Fear, I know thee by my throbbing heart,
> Thy withering power inspired each mournful line,
> Though gentle Pity claim her mingled part,
> Yet all the thunders of the scene are thine!

This was beauty such as Goethe saw in the Roman depiction of the Medusa head known as the Medusa Rondanini, a depiction that

Antonio Canova, *Perseus Holding the Severed Head of Medusa*, 1805, marble.

expresses 'the discord between death and life, between pain and pleasure, [and] exerts an inexplicable fascination over us as no other ambiguous figure does'. The Medusa Rondanini was used by the Italian sculptor Antonio Canova in his famous statue of Perseus holding up Medusa's severed head.

At the centre of the Romantic vision of Medusa are two exceptional creative works: a painting of the dead Medusa head attributed

A Flemish School head of Medusa, wrongly attributed to Leonardo da Vinci, *c.* 1600.

to Leonardo da Vinci but actually by a seventeenth-century Flemish artist; and a poem from the early nineteenth century by Percy Bysshe Shelley based on that painting.

It is of interest to note some of the circumstances surrounding the painting of the Medusa head that Leonardo apparently did complete but that was eventually lost, leading some to assume wrongly that the Flemish painting was his. According to the painter and art historian Giorgio Vasari, Leonardo's father, Piero, commissioned his son to paint something on a buckler belonging to one of his peasant workers. Leonardo agreed and decided to paint a face that would terrify anyone who saw it. He had in mind something equivalent to Medusa's head and its terrifying effect, and created a monstrous figure exuding steam, surrounded by serpents, locusts, bats and other beasts. After a time Leonardo told his father that the painting was complete and that he should come to fetch it. When Piero saw the painting on the buckler, he was dumbfounded – *médusé*, as the French would have said. Leonardo was delighted with his Medusa effect.

The painting that inspired Shelley was itself sufficiently gruesome to petrify. Walter Pater found 'the fascination of corruption' in it.

But what Shelley sees in the painting in his fragmentary poem 'On the Medusa of Leonardo da Vinci in the Florentine Gallery' (1819) is pure Romanticism.

It lieth, gazing on the midnight sky,
    Upon the cloudy mountain peak supine;
Below, far lands are seen tremblingly;
    Its horror and its beauty are divine.
Upon its lips and eyelids seems to lie
    Loveliness like a shadow, from which shrine,
Fiery and lurid, struggling underneath,
    The agonies of anguish and of death.

Yet it is less the horror than the grace
    Which turns the gazer's spirit into stone;
Whereon the lineaments of that dead face
    Are graven, till the characters be grown
Into itself, and thought no more can trace;
    'Tis the melodious hue of beauty thrown
Athwart the darkness and the glare of pain,
Which humanize and harmonize the strain.

And from its head as from one body grow,
    As [   ] grass out of a watery rock,
Hairs which are vipers, and they curl and flow
    And their long tangles in each other lock,
And with unending involutions shew
    Their mailed radiance, as it were to mock
The torture and the death within, and saw
The solid air with many a ragged jaw.

And from a stone beside, a poisonous eft
    Peeps idly into those Gorgonian eyes;
Whilst in the air a ghastly bat, bereft
    Of sense, has flitted with a mad surprise
Out of the cave this hideous light had cleft,
    And he comes hastening like a moth that hies

After a taper; and the midnight sky
Flares, a light more dread than obscurity.

'Tis the tempestuous loveliness of terror;
For from the serpents gleams a brazen glare
Kindled by that inextricable error,
Which makes a thrilling vapour of the air
Become a [ ] and ever-shifting mirror
Of all the beauty and the terror there –
A woman's countenance, with serpent locks,
Gazing in death on heaven from those wet rocks.

Quite recently an added stanza has been discovered:

It is a woman's countenance divine
With everlasting beauty breathing there
Which from a stormy mountain's peak, supine
Gazes into the night's trembling air.
It is a trunkless head, and on its feature
Death has met life, but there is life in death,
The blood is frozen – but unconquered Nature
Seems struggling to the last – without a breath
The fragment of an uncreated creature.

Like John Keats in his more famous 'Ode on a Grecian Urn', Shelley here chooses the method of ekphrasis, the attempt to recreate in poetry the essence of a painting, just as Leonardo in his lost buckler painting of Medusa had tried – apparently successfully – to recreate the power of the Medusa head. For Leonardo it was paint, for Shelley the word – the power of language to captivate the reader's soul – as Medusa's gaze had turned men to stone. A perfect example of the Roman poet Horace's famous epigram *ut pictura poesis* (as is painting, so is poetry), the poem, like the painting, is of course the protective mirror that allows us to experience the Medusa power without risk to our lives. As such it is for the reader the equivalent of Odysseus being tied to his mast so that he can experience the lure of the Sirens without being destroyed by their power.

The first stanza conveys the Romantic conflation of the horrible and the beautiful and the fascination with the ultimate experience, death. The dead Medusa head, eyes open, is 'gazing on the midnight sky . . . Its horror and its beauty are divine'. And, as in the case of Prometheus, another Romantic favourite victim figure, the Medusa struggles against the powers that killed her: from underneath her 'loveliness . . . fiery and lurid, struggling underneath' that gaze are 'the agonies of anguish and death'.

In the second stanza the poet presents what is, in effect, the new Romantic Medusa: 'it is less the horror than the grace / Which turns the gazer's spirit into stone'. The new Medusa's power comes from her grace rather than from any evil, and its target is not the body but the spirit – the soul. A Romantic Gorgoneion, this Medusa's beauty in the face of darkness and pain can 'humanize and harmonize the strain'.

In the third stanza the vipers and other figures surrounding Medusa are the forces against which the Gorgon struggles as the innocent victim. They 'mock / The torture and death within'. They are the punishment inflicted on the innocent by the arbitrary and corrupt forces of the status quo.

The fourth stanza speaks again to the Romantic fascination with the conflation of apparent opposites. The crucial line is the first: ''Tis the tempestuous loveliness of terror'. In this moment of terror that is her decapitation, the Medusa – the victim – is once again characterized by the gentle word 'loveliness'. And with 'all the beauty and terror there', the beautiful dead Medusa gazes defiantly 'on heaven from those wet rocks', becoming the essence of the Romantic hero-victim.

The final stanza, the recently discovered fragment first published and discussed by Neville Rogers, paves the way for future feminist admirers of the Gorgon: 'It is a woman's countenance divine / With everlasting beauty breathing there.' It is a 'trunkless head' but on its face we see that 'Death has met life, but there is life in death'. In the image of this Medusa, the defiant beautiful victim, 'unconquered Nature / Seems struggling to the last' – a creature waiting to be created, the mother, as we know, of the winged Pegasus, symbol of a new power and creative energy.

In the Victorian age the Pre-Raphaelite movement continued and developed the Romantic tradition of the beautiful Medusa victim. Dante Gabriel Rossetti (1828–1882) wrote 'Aspecta Medusa (for a Drawing)' about the Medusa head:

Andromeda, by Perseus sav'd and wed,
Hanker'd each day to see the Gorgon's head:
Till o'er a fount he held it, bade her lean,
And mirror'd in the wave was safely seen
That death she liv'd by.

Let not thine eyes know
Any forbidden thing itself, although
It once should save as well as kill: but be
Its shadow upon life enough for thee.

A painting by a fellow Pre-Raphaelite, Edward Burne-Jones, is an apt illustration for the poem. The head resting in the tree, though it has to be viewed in the reflecting fountain because of its power to turn gazers to stone, seems anything but ugly, and the lovers, Perseus and Andromeda, anything but fearful as they gaze at the reflection of the beautiful face. It is, of course, the painter and the poet rather than the original mythmakers who provide this vision of the Medusa's Romantic 'loveliness'.

That loveliness is perpetuated in Rossetti's own painting, entitled *Aspecta Medusa.* If the artist intended this painting to be of Medusa before her beheading (some have claimed that it is rather of Andromeda gazing into the fountain at Medusa's head), the poet has moved us back in time to the beautiful Medusa we have never seen but only heard of in the old myths – the Medusa as maiden, desired by Poseidon and later punished by Athene for her beauty. She seems wistful or sad, more the victim than the monster. Stripped of the vipers and the gruesomeness, she represents the gentle Pre-Raphaelite version of the Romantic vision, a version expressed by Rossetti when he wrote of his intention to create in his painting 'a pure ideal' without 'the least degree of . . . repugnant reality'. At its worst this Pre-Raphaelite treatment of

Edward Burne-Jones, *The Baleful Head*, 1887, oil on canvas.

Medusa turns her into what Kent Patterson calls 'the heroine of a sentimental best-seller'.

Perhaps the most famous work in which the Medusa name appeared in the Romantic age was the painting *The Raft of the Medusa* by the French painter Théodore Géricault (1791–1824). The work achieved fame as soon as it was exhibited. It depicts the raft on which 147 people experienced Medusa-like horror, including starvation and cannibalism, during thirteen days at sea after the beaching of the French naval warship *Méduse* in 1810.

It is indicative of the romanticizing of the monstrous Gorgon that the French Navy would name a frigate *Méduse*. A ship name such as *Hercules* or *Perseus* would be more in keeping with the heroic goals of a military establishment. The name *Méduse* suggests pain, ugliness and the perversion of nature – unless in the Romantic mode it connotes beautiful victimhood, still not a particularly apt name for a warship. In his painting, Géricault, working two years after the tragic wreck, manages to romanticize through his painterly powers the monstrous – highly realistic – sufferings of the raft victims. The figures are realistic but the overall painting appeals to the Romantic predilection for pain, storms and human victimhood. Medusa here is reincarnated as the raft and its tortured passengers. But by placing the elements of the tragedy in a spectacularly beautiful painting,

Dante Gabriel Rossetti, *Aspecta Medusa*, 1867, chalk.

Theodore Géricault, *The Raft of the Medusa*, 1819, oil on canvas.

the painter creates an Athene-style protective mirror which allows us to gaze at Medusa without danger of being permanently immobilized. Painterly skill allows us to escape disaster. Horror is turned into beauty. Although a Romantic icon, *The Raft of the Medusa*, with its graphically realistic elements, serves as a preface to the life of Medusa as understood in the age of realism.

V

Medusa in the Age of Realism

The face of modernity.
Walter Benjamin

During the period between the Victorian age and our own, Medusa became primarily a symbol for various elements in the universally focused theories and intellectual conversations that dominate the era. The myth itself is no longer the central concern. Her head remains central, as always, but it no longer represents horror, female depravity, the femme fatale, Romantic victimization or a particular culture.

Medusa's Head as Symbol

The seventeenth-century philosopher Francis Bacon might be seen as a precursor to the realist interpreters of the Medusa myth. In his *The Wisdom of the Ancients* (1609) he sees the story of Perseus and Medusa as an allegory for the proper rules of warfare. So it is, for instance, that Perseus, by choosing the Gorgon, who was mortal, for his target, chose a war that was possible to win. The fact that he finds Medusa asleep suggests that the true warrior tries to attack his enemy when the latter is not expecting him. Here in the age of realism, Medusa loses any particular personality but takes on a symbolic mantle of importance that encompasses anthropology, history, philosophy, politics and, above all, psychology.

The Blood of Medusa, a drawing of 1898 by the Belgian Symbolist Fernand Khnopff, captures something of the new Medusa. The eyes stare coldly straight ahead. The mouth is calm and determined. This Medusa is fearless. Her head is supported by a neck that resembles a metal collar, giving it an almost industrial look. Snakes lurch out

Fernand Khnopff, *The Blood of Medusa*, 1898, pencils on paper.

from the head in a menacing manner. Out of her blood springs the flying horse Pegasus. This is a Medusa conveying a sense of resurrected power for a new age.

The Khnopff drawing would be a perfect illustration of what Karl Marx in his *Capital* (1867) saw in the Medusa head. For Marx, the Gorgon head was a symbol of the monstrous evils of capitalism itself, evils that society tends to ignore. The 'social statistics' of Western Europe, he wrote, 'raise the veil just enough to let us catch a glimpse of the Medusa head behind it'. But just as Perseus wore a cap of invisibility, 'we draw the magic cap down over eyes and ears as a make-believe that there are no monsters'.

In *The Birth of Tragedy* (1872), Friedrich Nietzsche sees the Medusa head as a symbol of the Apollonian struggle against rampant Dionysianism: 'the figure of Apollo, rising full of pride, held out the Gorgon's head to this grotesquely uncouth Dionysian power'. Here 'Apollonian', from the Greek god of sun and light, refers to order, form, structure and reason in art and life; 'Dionysian', from the god of wine and ecstasy, to the creative, intuitive and emotional powers. Bernard Pautrat in his essay 'Nietzsche Médusé' points out that in one of his drafts for his *Thus Spake Zarathustra*, Nietzsche referred to Medusa's head as the 'Great Thought', presumably the thought of the Eternal Return, the philosopher's theory that 'the eternal hourglass of existence is turned over again and again'. Certainly Medusa over the centuries has returned in many guises and functions.

Jane Harrison and other scholars of anthropology in the so-called Myth and Ritual School at Cambridge in the late nineteenth and early twentieth centuries were interested in Medusa, particularly in connection with the symbolic power of her severed head. Harrison points out that it is only when the head is severed from the body that it gains its particular power as a Gorgoneion (although it must be said that her stare itself had always been able to turn victims to stone). The severed head, as has been demonstrated earlier, is an ancient motif, perhaps having its source, as ritualists have suggested, in sacrificial fertility rituals in which the severed head is that of the *pharmakos* or ritual scapegoat whose blood must be spilled to redeem the whole community. In many myths – the Welsh myth of Bran, for example – a severed head continues to speak, suggesting that it is the head rather than the body or heart that houses the soul. The blood from the severed head is both dangerous and regenerative. Spilled, the Gorgon's blood produces vipers, but out of her blood also springs the proud Pegasus. For the archaeologist Marija Gimbutas, the Gorgon's head is representative of the 'dynamic life energy' of the Mother Goddess. For other ritualists, Medusa is more a symbol of the human faith in the efficacy of sacrifice for the good of all.

The Psychoanalytic Medusa

Of all the disciplines concerned with the Medusa symbol during the post-Victorian period, it is the new science of psychoanalysis that stands out. In the works of Sigmund Freud, Carl Jung and their followers, the Medusa figure gains whole new sets of clothes, clothes that would have confused Hesiod, Homer and Apollodorus and horrified the painters and poets of the Middle Ages, the Renaissance and the Romantic age.

In 1922 Freud wrote his essay 'Medusa's Head' (published posthumously in 1940), in which he linked the Medusa head with a theory regarding fear of castration. He begins by centring on the part of the Medusa myth that involves the separation of the head from the body – the decapitation. Decapitation, he postulates, is simply a symbol for castration. He suggests that the terror arising from Medusa's decapitation is really a fear of castration and that castration is tied to the immobilizing sight of something. That something, he proposes, based on 'numerous analyses', is the female genitals – almost always the mother's genitals. Boys, he claims, are frequently threatened with castration, but the threat becomes real only when a boy happens to see his mother's genitals 'surrounded by shocking hair' and lacking the familiar penis. If the mother is 'castrated', he can be too.

Freud goes on to remind us that in the Medusa head the hair is replaced by snakes, which must also be related to the 'castration complex'. The snakes are clearly phallic – they replace the missing penis – but the chaotic multiple penises also represent castration. (According to Freud, 'a multiplication of penis symbols signifies castration.') However, in the myth exposure to the Medusa's head 'makes the spectator stiff with terror'; that is, 'turns him to stone'. This process of 'becoming stiff . . . means an erection', reminding the person involved in the castration complex that he still has a penis.

The 'unapproachable', anti-sexual Athene, says Freud, is in effect castrated. She carries the image of the Medusa head – really the image of the female genitals – to terrify enemies. Thus the Medusa that is horrifying to the individual can be used apotropaically against the enemy. In the same way the erect penis 'has an apotropaic effect', reminding others that one is not castrated. The person with the erection says, basically, 'I am not afraid of you. I defy you. I have a penis.' One thinks here of Perseus with his special sword approaching the terrifying Medusa.

In the essay 'The Infantile Genital Organization' (1923), Freud claims that homosexuality and the demeaning of women stem from 'the conviction that women have no penis'. In 'Fetishism' (1927) he maintains that 'probably no male human being is spared the fright of castration at the sight of the female genitals'. Finally, in the first essay he reminds us that the neurologist Sándor Ferenczi, in his 'On the Symbolism of the Head of Medusa' (1923), wrote that the head of Medusa is clearly a symbol of the female genitals without a penis. Like Freud, Ferenczi, in his essay, suggests that the presence of snakes surrounding the Medusa head somehow emphasizes the lack of a penis and thus compounds the terror of the child fearing castration. The Medusa's 'alarming' eyes for Ferenczi 'have the secondary meaning of erection'. It is worth noting, as the sociologist Philip Slater points out, that petrifaction here might just as well be symbolic of impotence: 'While Freud [and Ferenczi] focuses on stiffness', say Slater, 'we can just as well stress the numb or anesthetic aspect of turning to stone'.

Carl Jung and his followers have a less sexually oriented understanding of Medusa and her myth. Their concern is with the universal psychic tendencies – the archetypes – it reveals. In *Archetypes and the Collective Unconscious* (*CW* IX, 2: 193–212), Jung discusses the 'Medusa effect', the psychic petrification that can occur when the patient is confronted with a seemingly impossible situation and cannot deal with it alone. He compares this effect to that of the jellyfish sting, the jellyfish also being called the Medusa fish. Medusa in the myth has the Freudian sexual side, but just as the jellyfish is, like the Virgin Mary, the *stella maris*, the star of the sea, she also has a spiritual side; the high and the low exist together as opposites within her. For Jung the Medusa in us all is the sometimes chaotic element which has the potential both for creativity and destruction.

Others might have referred to this aspect as the Dionysian side of the personality. To avoid destruction – in psychological terms, extreme psychosis or schizophrenia – we must follow the example of Perseus, who looked at Medusa only in a reflection, reflection here encompassing the idea of mental reflection, a practice more Apollonian than Dionysian.

Jungians in general see Medusa and her tormentor, Athene, as two archetypal images primarily connected with women. Athene is the non-sexual aspect representing dominant male priorities. She is the aspect of the woman as protector of patriarchal control. Medusa can only be seen in connection with Athene. Medusa is the chaotic, erotic and uncontrollable aspect of the woman. The psychologist Eric Neumann suggested in *The Great Mother* (1963) that she is the 'devouring chasm' of the ancient Great Mother which Perseus, as the hero of the new patriarchal age, must confront with the help of Hermes and Athene, 'the tutelary deities of wisdom and consciousness'. When finally 'possessed' sexually by the male – as represented by Poseidon in the myth – the woman becomes a being divided between two impulses, represented by Athene and Medusa. Perseus is the ego force – the persona – who must find the balance between the two sides.

The Philosophical Medusa

Psychoanalysis, then, provided one alternative approach to the earlier interpretations of Medusa. A more nihilistic alternative in the age of realism suggests that the Medusa's horrifying and destructive stare represents a revelation of the meaninglessness of life. To escape that meaninglessness – that 'Medusa truth' – we live a lie. As a character in Jack London's novel *The Mutiny of Elsinore* (1914) puts it:

> The profoundest instinct in man is to war against the truth; that is, against the Real. He shuns facts from his infancy. His life is a perpetual evasion. Miracle, chimera and to-morrow keep him alive. He lives on fiction and myth. It is the Lie that makes him free . . . The animal, awake, has no fictional escape from the Real because he has no imagination. Man,

> awake, is compelled to seek a perpetual escape into Hope, Belief, Fable, Art, God, Socialism, Immortality, Alcohol, Love. From Medusa-Truth he makes an appeal to Maya-lie [illusion].

In *Being and Nothingness* (1943), Jean-Paul Sartre brings Medusa into his world of existentialist philosophy. The 'petrifaction in in-itself by the Other', he says, 'is the profound meaning of the myth of Medusa'. The Other here is any person who looks at another, making the recipient of the look, the 'in-itself', feel objectified – de-individualized – to the extent that his 'subjectivity' has been petrified. Medusa represents the objectifying look, the gaze, of the Other, that which objectifies and takes away Self. If one looks at something, Sartre says, the one who looks is the centre of consciousness. The one who looks controls the world of the particular scene. But if, while looking, the looker is looked on by another, he becomes not only a being in and for itself but an objectified self for the Other. In this case, the self that belongs to the recipient of the look is different from the self seen by the Other, and, as Hazel Barnes in 'The Look of the Gorgon' (1974) explains: 'The Other's Look reveals to me that I am not alone in the world.' That might be all right in itself, until I realize that now '*the* world is no longer *my* world.' In short, the Other's look might deny 'my own freely organized world' and therefore 'reduce me permanently to a hard stonelike object'. The only solution to this problem is to assert one's existence by making the self-defining choice of looking at the Other and in so doing neutralizing what is symbolized by the Gorgon's life-denying look. This is the existentialist's understanding of the only possible role of the post-Romantic alienated individual.

The artists and thinkers in the Middle Ages and the Renaissance adapted Medusa to their particular priorities, interpreting her as a femme fatale having to do with sin as opposed to Christian virtues, and the Romantic painters and poets remade her to fit their ideals of beauty and the struggle against tyranny. Great thinkers of the age of realism – Marx, Nietzsche, Freud, Jung, Sartre – stripped the Medusa myth of its magic, of its superstition, and applied it to what they saw, not as ideals or as a war of conflicting values, but as reality.

For Marx the evils of capitalism were evident for all to see. For Nietzsche the Dionysian-Apollonian struggle *was* reality. For Freud and Jung the power of the unconscious and of inner demons were as real as the patients on their couches. For Sartre, the Medusa's stare stood for an existential reality that is basic to human society. Once a mysterious and terrifying monster central to a myth seen from many perspectives, the new Medusa had come into her own as a symbolic reality operating at the very centre of modern life. The critic Walter Benjamin saw in Medusa's look 'the face of modernity itself', which 'blasts us with its immemorial gaze'.

VI
The Modern Intellectual Medusa

The Gorgon's head is nothing more than a mask.
Roger Caillois

In the second half of the twentieth century Medusa fascinated the most avant-garde intellectuals. She became an aesthetic symbol, a representation of conventional attitudes, material culture and the Other, and a metaphor for aspects of structuralism, deconstruction and postmodernism in general. Why did this somewhat obscure classical monster become so central to the thoughts of intellectuals, and then, later, to the key figures of extreme contemporary culture. The answer seems to lie in her capacity for complexity, her ability to speak to so many interests at once. She can be the Other so necessary to the existentialist, the composite metaphor for the analysand so important to the psychoanalyst, and an appropriately complex symbol and starting point for the intricate theories of professional intellectuals.

Medusa and the French Intellectuals

Medusa has been a particular favourite of several of the major post-Second World War French intellectuals. These thinkers have used Medusa freely in a metaphorical manner to illustrate particular theories, and in some cases have presumed to alter the myth or to add new elements to it to support those theories. Some of the most prominent French thinkers have drawn on the Medusa myth, including the philosopher-critics Roland Barthes, Jacques Derrida, Roger Caillois and Louis Marin, the scholar of religion Jean-Pierre Vernant and the mythologist Françoise Frontisi-Ducroux.

In his autobiography *Roland Barthes* (1975), the structuralist Barthes equates what he calls 'Doxa', conventional opinion or common beliefs, with Medusa. Both lead to petrifaction. It is true, he writes, that there are beautiful elements in Doxa. But Doxa exists as if nothing had taken place since its inception. That is, Doxa is composed of thoughts that were once useful but are now useless. These once beautiful ideas are now sleeping and turned into caricature by true wisdom, represented in the myth by Medusa's enemy, Athene. As a writer, Barthes sees himself as necessarily excluded from the language of Doxa yet condemned to listen to it and thus to be frozen or petrified by its oppressive presence. It might be said that Barthes' dilemma is the one that faces all artists and writers: the problem of breaking through the conventional to communicate something original. This is the dilemma faced also by heroes like Perseus, who must take up the challenge of the impossible – obtaining the Medusa head – in order to achieve self-definition or herohood.

It can be argued that Barthes' Doxa theory tells us more about Doxa than about Medusa. The biographer must ask whether there is anything in the Medusa myth to suggest the Gorgon as the sleeping of a once beautiful idea. The idea of a conflict between conventionalism and the artist's vision does, however, shed some light on the nature of Perseus' quest for Medusa's head. Artists have always had to struggle against the demands of the expected in order to reveal something original or unexpected.

Still more complex is the deconstructionist treatment of Medusa by Jacques Derrida in his book *Glas* (1974). In the course of deconstructing G.W.F. Hegel's discussion in the essay 'The Spirit of Christianity and Its Fate' (1798–9) of the importance of circumcision and the sacrifice of Isaac in Judaism, Derrida – himself a secular Jew – takes note of Hegel's use of Medusa as a metaphor for an aspect of Judaism itself. For Hegel, by seeing themselves as the 'chosen' and thus self-segregated people of God, everyone and everything else in the world becomes to Jews mere matter: 'the Gorgon's head transformed everything to stone.' Sounding something like Sartre in his discussion of the Other, Derrida explains that for Hegel, the Jew, 'like the Gorgon . . . materializes, petrifies everything he sees and everything that regards him'. Turning to Hegel's treatment of circumcision and the sacrifice of Isaac, Derrida seems to return to the Freudian vision of Medusa. In the act of circumcision and the sacrifice, 'the Jew effects on himself a simulacrum of castration in order to mark his ownness . . . and to constitute himself as the favourite slave of the infinite power'. His castration/circumcision becomes in itself apotropaic, a Medusa's head, an 'erection that defies the other'. The Derrida approach adds a dimension to the Freudian one and is perhaps a contribution to the understanding of Judaism, but does it tell the biographer anything significant about Medusa?

Louis Marin's comments on Medusa in his *Détruire la peinture* ('To Destroy Painting', 1977) are centred on the famous Caravaggio painting of the Gorgon. In the course of a highly theoretical discourse on the nature of painting, Marin indulges in what is in effect a retelling – some might say a distortion – of the Medusa myth. He considers the Caravaggio painting as an act of ekphrasis, in this case the painting of a story. He notes the importance of the single shared eye in the myth, for instance, regarding it as a symbol of the act of seeing so important in painting as well as in the myth, but he confuses the Graiae, the possessors of the single eye, with the two Gorgon sisters of Medusa. He also has a theory about the effect of the mirror on Medusa herself which is not evident in the myth. Through the ruse of the mirror – a trickery of sight – he says, Perseus not only avoids looking at Medusa but creates a representation – a painting, as it were – of Medusa in the mirror. And in so doing he tricks Medusa into looking at herself, which causes her to turn to stone just at the instant her head is removed.

Roger Caillois in *Méduse et compagnie* (1960, English title *The Mask of the Medusa*) had suggested that Perseus uses the mirror to 'reflect to the monster her own fascinating face', in effect creating an amuletic mask, the Gorgoneion. Françoise Frontisi-Ducroux, in 'The Gorgon, Paradigm of Image Creation' (1993), also sees the Medusa head as a representation in ancient Greek life of the 'unspeakable horror of death' which, when projected onto the viewer, in effect, petrifies him. The moment of decapitation is for Marin, as it had been for Caillois, a moment of 'singular metamorphosis . . . when the Gorgon's violence is immobilized in its very expression, imprinting itself on itself'. It is the moment when Medusa is captured 'in the trap of her own deadly gaze', the moment in which she is *médusé*.

The subject of Caravaggio's painting, Marin asserts, is 'the gaze'. We see the Medusa's gaze at the instant of death before she can even give voice to her pain. The Medusa's gaze cannot find us – or the invisible Perseus. It impossible to engage the gaze of the Medusa with one's own gaze as one would normally do with a full-face portrait. She looks down and away. She sees nothing but transparency where we are or where Perseus is, and this makes the observer into nothing. All the Medusa sees is herself in the mirror; she is the embodiment here of narcissism at the very moment when, like Narcissus gazing at himself in the pool, she falls into death. In the painting, says Marin, the painter's own gaze has captured the 'infinitesimal moment during which she has just looked at herself and is no longer doing so'.

Marin here is following in the tradition of Shelley and others who attempt to recreate a painting in words and is giving the attempt a particularly modernist effect by concentrating on the creative process revealed in the painting itself. In their discussions, Marin and Caillois both make significant alterations to the mythic events described by the original 'witnesses' to the Medusa story. The biographer can only be wary of such alterations. The question for the biographer here is whether a myth exists and must be examined as told in the particular period of its admittedly gradual development, or whether the narrative element of a myth continues to develop over time along with the interpretations of it, making the 'facts' of the story as told for one culture quite different from those told by another. Is it reasonable to assume that the classical myth as told by Homer, Hesiod, Apollodorus and Ovid contains the relatively homogeneous 'facts' of Medusa's life, or must we argue that these 'facts' can be changed by thinkers of another age?

Jean-Pierre Vernant picks up on the work of these earlier critics in his *Mortals and Immortals* (1991), a collection of essays including 'Death in the Eyes: Gorgo Figure of the Other' and 'In the Mirror of Medusa' (both 1985). Vernant examines Medusa – the Gorgo – in the context of archaic Greek religious life. Always depicted in frontal rather than profile pose and always monstrous, Medusa for Vernant is essentially a mask conveying the ultimate Other. She represents that death power which 'wrenches humans away from their lives'. To gaze at the Other which is the Medusa mask is to lose the self, to be petrified. Furthermore, to face the Gorgo mask in archaic ritual was to face one's own double – the Other in oneself, the dark side. In short, what the Gorgo allows one to see when one meets her gaze is 'yourself in the world beyond'.

Here the critic, building on Sartre's idea of Medusa and the Other, brings an original interpretation to the 'facts' of the myth, one that does not alter events to fit a theory but that adds a significant element to the meaning of Medusa, the connection between the Medusa and the self.

Other Views

It is not only French scholars who have made use of the Medusa myth to support particular theories. An American professor of English literature, Neil Hertz, takes a somewhat original approach to Medusa, considering the Medusa head in the context of the French Revolution as 'a representation of what would seem to be a political threat as if it were a sexual threat'. He begins his argument by pointing back to Freud's theory involving a boy child's fear of castration when he sees his mother's genitals and realizes that she has no penis. And he remembers that later, in his essay on fetishism, Freud suggested that 'in later life grown men may experience a similar panic [Hertz calls it 'hysteria'], when the cry goes up that throne and altar are in danger'. Thus sexuality and politics overlap. Hertz points out that Victor Hugo told how, at the beginning of the French Revolution of 1848, two prostitutes stood on the barricades, lifted their dresses to expose their mid-sections and insulted the National Guard soldiers, who immediately shot them. This chilling act of blatant sexual exposure in which, according to the Freudian view, the women reminded the men of their possible castration, leads Hertz back to the Medusa and the head that is held up as a threatening apotropaic talisman, as on the shield of Athene and the great statues by Cellini and Canova of Perseus holding up the head. For Hertz, as for Freud, the Gorgon becomes once again a petrifying force, reducing men to hysteria based on a sexual fear of the defiant female body – a fear of 'enslavement, seduction, and the loss of manhood'.

Another professor, Tobin Siebers, in his book *The Mirror of Medusa* (1983), takes up the question of mirroring, doubling and narcissism where the French critics Louis Marin and Roger Caillois left off. Siebers sees the eye as a crucial element in the Perseus-Medusa myth. It is the eye of the Graiae that, at least indirectly, leads Perseus to Medusa and makes him invisible to her, which allows him to gain the talismanic head – the petrifying stare of the Gorgon – to use as a protection against the evil eye itself. In short, in the Medusa head we have the 'emblem of the stupefying look', the origin of the Gorgoneion in particular and all amulets in general. Such amulets often take the form of eyes.

Siebers agrees with Caillois' and Marin's suggestion that Medusa sees herself in the 'mirror' of Perseus' shield and dies as a result. The shield, then, with its image of the Medusa (an image later attached to the shield of Athene), is a de facto amulet against the evil eye. By seeing herself and dying, Medusa, like Narcissus seeing himself in the pool and dying, becomes an emblem of narcissism, narcissism being ultimately a cause of petrifaction, an inability to function in life. The murder of Medusa is at once a curse and a sanctifying sacrifice. The evil eye becomes the defence against the evil eye. Evil is mirrored to defeat evil. Siebers postulates that the evolution of Medusa from monster to beautiful victim over the centuries suggests that she and Athene are in fact masks of the same being. In this assertion, hinted at earlier by Jane Harrison and the Jungians, he notes, as had Harrison, that snakes are associated with both figures. It was Athene, often accompanied by snakes, who replaced Medusa's hair with snakes.

The association of Athene and Medusa as aspects of the same being and the connection between Medusa and narcissism – a connection noted earlier in our discussions of the *Roman de la rose* and of Petrarch – provides the biographer with an insight that adds to the essential question behind any biography: what does this life have to do with my life? Again, this is a question that will be basic to the biographer's conclusions.

In his article 'The Medusa Complex: A Theory of Stoned Posthumanism' (2005) the Canadian theorist Ted Hiebert provides a different view of Medusa's gaze . Hiebert sees the famous gaze of

Medusa as 'a convincing metaphor for the liberal humanist gaze – at essence an objectifying gaze, a gaze that constitutes its subjects according to rules, most often unchosen by them, but which never-the-less become the communal basis of Western living'. Furthermore, Hiebert believes the metaphor of the gaze works just as well for the 'postmodern gaze' that petrifies through 'intellectual paralysis of uncertain subjectivity'. Like the French intellectuals, Hiebert asks, in the spirit of post-humanism, 'What would happen when Medusa looks into the mirror and confronts herself in the deadly gaze of her own vision?' This is the Medusa complex, the way of 'perceiving and believing' that changes our perception of the world through its denial of 'traditional boundaries'. The Medusa complex makes these boundaries 'fictional'. As in the cases of some of the French critics, the biographer is faced here with an admittedly original and interesting *use* of Medusa rather than with information about who Medusa is. As far as we know, Medusa did not look into the mirror. It was Perseus who did so.

Stephen Wilk, an American physicist, examines Medusa in meticulous detail in his *Medusa: Solving the Mystery of the Gorgon* (2000). He suggests many possibilities for the solving of Medusa's meaning. One suggestion stems from the fact that Homer and other tellers of the myth place the Gorgon in the Land of the Dead. The Medusa head as traditionally depicted, with its protruding tongue, wild eyes and bloated face, is seen as a possible depiction of a 'putrefying corpse'. Wilk points to parallel figures in world mythology which support this hypothesis. The Indian goddess Kali lives among the dead and shares many facial characteristics with Medusa. The Mexican Mictecuhtli, lord of the dead, like his consort Mictecacihuatl, discussed earlier, has the Gorgon grimace and protruding tongue. Wilk also reminds us of the ancient custom of beheading criminals and displaying their decomposing heads on stakes for all to view. Such displays suggest an apotropaic intention, warning people against crime. In short, the severed head becomes a socially petrifying Gorgoneion. Another possible explanation for the distorted Gorgon head, says Wilk, is a form 'just as universal as death and decay': 'the appearance of a human being undergoing a hysterical fit' or experiencing madness.

Wilk's explanation perhaps explains an aspect of the depictions of the Medusa head and the heads of related figures from other cultures, but, again, it does not lead the biographer to a vision of Medusa herself. Like Wilk and others, the Harvard professor Marjorie Garber takes up the severed head theme in her 'Macbeth: The Male Medusa' (1987). When Macduff brings in the head of the defeated Macbeth at the end of Shakespeare's *Macbeth*, the head is 'presented as if in allegorical tableau'. Metaphorically speaking, the audience is inevitably 'turned to stone' – at least 'taken aback' – by the appearance of the bloody head. The severed head of the 'monster' king 'is transformed from an emblem of evil to a token of good', an 'object lesson in tyranny' for all to see. This contribution to our understanding of the Medusa head as an apotropaic talisman, a Gorgoneion, is both original and useful.

In summary then, although the biographer must consider discussions of Medusa wherever they are to be found, he must consider whether these discussions contribute significantly to our understanding of Medusa's true identity. In some cases the critics have provided insights. But the biographer must, of course, wonder whether apparent additions to or alterations of the original myth tell more about the new mythmakers, their intellectual priorities and the demands and assumptions of their postmodernist milieu than they do about the subject of the biography. The same question must apply to the feminist approach to Medusa, which has dominated Medusa interest in the contemporary intellectual world.

VII

The Feminist Medusa

She's beautiful and she's laughing.
Hélène Cixous

The earliest indication of a feminist view of Medusa is found in *Le Livre de la cité des dames* ('The Book of the City of Ladies', 1405) by Christine de Pizan, a French-Italian writer of the late Middle Ages who was concerned with women's issues. While others of the period warned of the evil represented by Medusa, Christine claimed that it was really the Gorgon's extreme beauty that turned people to stone, that is, made them 'immovable'. For Christine the snakes in Medusa's hair become beautiful golden curls, and Medusa becomes a worthy inhabitant of the city of admirable ladies.

It is the French poet, philosopher and literary critic Hélène Cixous who has most famously expressed the modern feminist view of Medusa. Cixous' career as a post-structuralist feminist came to full fruition in 1975 with the publication of her article 'Le Rire de la Méduse' ('The Laugh of the Medusa'). For some time Cixous had linked questions of sexuality with language and other forms of social communication, and in the Medusa essay the Gorgon becomes a central metaphor in that linkage.

For Cixous, a woman's sexuality – her desires and longings – exist outside of the world's language and communication system, a system that, like Jacques Derrida, she sees as being phallogocentric or phallocentric, dominated by the phallus, the masculine-based concept of meaning. The result is the creation of guilt in the minds of women, guilt about sexual longings and activities such as masturbation. In a world in which the language of life is that of the phallocentric male, women have seen themselves as monstrous, as the Medusa traditionally depicted by males, the Medusa decapitated by the phallocentric Perseus.

Cixous' message to women is a rallying cry. The Medusa's world is not a dark one, and it is not unexplorable, as we have been made by the phallocentric language of life to think it is. Women are called not to turn their eyes from the Medusa within, not to look at her by way of mirrors. 'You have only to look at the Medusa straight on to see her. And she's not deadly. She's beautiful and laughing.' In this way the phallogocentric lie will be exposed.

Having been turned away from their own bodies, their own sexuality, having been made to be modest, women must now create a new language of life and in so doing free the female body and the laughing Medusa.

This beautiful Medusa – raped, decapitated, turned into a monster by men – is the same Medusa out of whose decapitated body sprang the winged horse Pegasus, beauty itself. Medusa did not turn others to stone; it was she who was victimized, made into a monster by the 'male gaze'. Men 'need femininity to be associated with death', says Cixous; 'it's the jitters that give them a hard-on! for themselves'. The old Medusa myth is a facade; Cixous' myth is the new, true story.

In short, the metamorphosis of the beautiful Medusa into a monster reflects the change women have undergone over the centuries from sexually whole to sexually incomplete beings. The old Medusa myth is one created by men and believed by women. It is time now, says Cixous, for women to free themselves of the old myth and to embrace the beautiful laughing Medusa.

In his essay 'Difference' (1978), using Medusa briefly as a feminist metaphor, the film theorist Stephen Heath, like Cixous, considers questions of female sexuality, looking and mirroring. In the 'language' of the phallocentric patriarchal society, he writes, women are trapped in a mirror:

> What then of the look for the woman, of woman subjects in seeing? The reply given by psychoanalysis is from the phallus. If the woman looks, the spectacle provokes, castration is in the air, the Medusa's head is not far off; thus she must not look, is absorbed herself on the side of the seen, seeing herself seeing herself.

The French feminist critic Sarah Kofman was deeply influenced by Derrida, Vernant and Marin as well as by Freud's understanding of the Medusa myth. In *The Enigma of Women: Women in Freud's Writing* (1980), she accepts Freud's and Ferenczi's association between the female genitals and the Medusa head, suggesting that 'woman's genital organs arouse an inseparable blend of horror and pleasure', both awakening and relieving castration anxiety. And, in her *Camera obscura: De l'idéologie* (1973), like Vernant and Marin, she takes up the idea of Medusa's seeing herself reflected in Perseus' shield. Perseus is able to overpower (*méduser*) Medusa with the gaze of her own image. That is to say, it is the artistic image of the Medusa that succeeds in overcoming the Gorgon herself. Perseus was the victor only because Medusa was both the petrifier and the petrified, both monstrous and beautiful. In short, Perseus turns the horror into art by means of the mirror-shield but can only do so because the true Medusa – like the female genitals – is already Apollonian, already the bearer of a beautiful therapeutic image.

The Italian feminist scholar Teresa de Lauretis, in her book *Alice Doesn't: Feminism, Semiotics, Cinema* (1984), builds on the revised myth explored earlier by Louis Marin, Jean-Pierre Vernant, Roger Caillois, Tobin Siebers, Sarah Kofman and Stephen Heath in which Medusa herself, not asleep as in the original myth, is frozen by her own mirrored image. De Lauretis suggests that women have metaphorically fallen asleep during the many cinematic slayings of Medusa 'from *Psycho* to *Blow Out*'. De Lauretis's question, referring back to Freud's question 'What does woman want?', is: what does Medusa – as woman – 'feel looking at herself being slain?' For De Lauretis this is a 'political question' having to do with the way we look at and see women. The Perseus-Medusa legend is important in this context because Medusa is a 'threat to man's vision'. Her 'power consists in [her] enigma and 'to be-looked-at-ness ... [her] luring of the man's gaze into the "dark continent", as Freud put it, the enigma of femininity'. In short, she is an obstacle man 'encounters on the path of life, on his way to manhood, wisdom and power'. As such, she 'must be slain or defeated so that he can go forward to fulfill his destiny'. Similarly, Susan Bowers in her essay 'Medusa and the Female Gaze' (1990) argues that in both the ancient and modern worlds Medusa has represented for men what they 'most feared: sensual and powerful women', who therefore had to be slain.

In 'The Voice of the Shuttle is Ours' (1984), Patricia Klindienst sees the rape of Medusa as a ritual sacrifice of the female on the altar of a goddess, Athene, who was born not of a woman but of Zeus and who was therefore not a real woman but 'a male fantasy of what a woman ought to be'. Medusa 'threatens men', Athene does not. As such, the rape of Medusa represents the silencing of women by the male-dominated culture.

Ann Stanford in her poem 'Medusa' (1977) focuses on the rape itself and, by extension, on the physical and psychological horrors of rape as well as the cultural imprisonment of women. In the poem we come perhaps as close as we ever have to what might have been the real feelings of Medusa in at least a part of her story. Using Medusa's voice, the poet describes the young woman's first sight of the god, an old man 'dripping with seaweed' emerging from the sea, climbing up the temple stairs where she stood. After praising her 'grace', the god rapes her, treats her roughly like a 'field hand'. Medusa's shocked reaction takes the form of pure hatred. Her hair coils into snakes and she thinks only of that form of revenge so much a signature of her story: 'my eyes saw the world in stone'. The former priestess of Athene becomes an agent of infertility; her mere glance 'destroyed all living things there'. Medusa now is a prisoner of her own rage, a 'prisoner of myself' longing for her old self. But memories of the god – his 'stinking breath', his 'sweaty weight' – make that longing fruitless. And the god's 'monster seed' imprisoned within her turns her 'blood to stone'.

Religion scholar Emily Erwin Culpepper in her 'Ancient Gorgons: A Face for Contemporary Women's Rage' (1986) sees the Gorgon head, the Gorgoneion, as a positive apotropaic emblem. Citing the feminist mythologist Barbara Walker and Robert Graves, she notes the connection between the Gorgon head and the Destroyer aspect of the ancient Triple Lunar Goddess. The Gorgoneian, she suggests, may have been worn by the goddess's priestesses to emphasize the deity's rage and destructive power. Pointing to the theory of many feminists that the Gorgons were representative of a black Amazon tribe hated by the Greeks, Culpepper reminds us that the 'Amazon Gorgon face is fury personified' and that the 'Gorgon/Medusa image has been rapidly adopted by large numbers of feminists who recognize her as one face of our own rage'.

Culpepper tells the story of her own successful defence against an attempted rape by means of karate and a face twisted into a Medusa-like 'fighting frenzy' which she glimpsed in a mirror as she fought off the rapist and, by extension, the patriarchy. 'Daily outrages against women', writes Culpepper, make it important to learn how to 'manifest a visage that will repel men when necessary'. The Gorgon face is not to be feared. May Sarton, in her poem 'The Muse as Medusa' (1971), goes so far as to see Medusa's face as 'my face', the reflection of 'frozen rage' which must be explored.

As an example of the Medusa face 'fulfilling the ancient Gorgon's function as guardian and promise of the female power within', Culpepper points to the painting of Medusa's face by Laura Kaye on the cover of lesbian feminist Elana Dykewomon's *They Will Know Me By My Teeth* (1976). In the same vein, Culpepper quotes a little poem by Anne Forfreedom:

Medusa of the Snakes

They used your name
to frighten us.
But you
don't frighten me.

They used your fame
to threaten us.
But you
don't threaten me.

The patriarchs wanted
to separate us.
And you
were their weapon.

No more this lie
No more this fear.

You belong
to us again.

Amazon queen
defender and healer
of women,
we claim you.

We call your name
to aid us.
and you
greet us anew.
Medusa! Medusa! Medusa!

In 'Who's Looking at Who(m): Re-viewing Medusa' (1996), Lizbeth Goodman describes the importance of the Medusa myth in the feminist theory, queer theory and black consciousness that informed much avant-garde theatre of the 1990s. As an example, she highlights the one-woman work *Medusa* by Dorothea Smartt, performed at the Institute of Contemporary Arts in London in 1993. Smartt reveals that a black woman's appearance and resulting self-identity stand in contrast to the 'cultural values' expressed in the appearance of white women. In effect the black woman becomes a mythic figure. The children in her Brixton neighbourhood of London call Smartt 'Medusa' because of her 'done up' hair – 'the curl, the kink, the happiness of black hair'. As a statement of her sense of otherness her hair is a symbol of power and sexuality. To change that hair, to make it more 'white', would be to 'unplug yourself from the power source'. Holding up a mirror both to herself and her audience, Smartt demands that the world return her gaze. 'Medusa was probably some black woman with nappy hair', she muses, 'and some white man saw her and cried: a monster'.

'A Navy Blue Afro' (1976), a poem by Colleen McElroy in which a black woman with an Afro is contrasted with black women who have 'their Medusa hair tamed', conveys an aspect of Smartt's message'.

I see her crossing the square
her hair

glinting like the midnight
of a blue Jamaican sky
she walks through the crowds
of ragged students
her hair oddly blue
her chin arched and poised
walking like some illustrated page
of today's woman
you have seen them
in their Rhine wine sunglasses
vying for visibility
for cover stories
you have seen them
all those fake Furies
coiffured
powdered
and costumed
their Medusa hair tamed
and dressed in new money
they are so rich
they piss in droplets
or fake it commenting
in cultured voice on the latest trivia
smiling always smiling
into the camera
you have seen them poised
and ready for a call to charity
microsex
unisex
jetsex
sometimes I can almost see
the girl with the navy blue hair
among them
until she turns
and her blackness sings to me
like a Jacob Lawrence painting.

An unusual feminist use of Medusa is to be found in an essay of 2009 by Amy Adler, a New York University law professor. In 'Medusa: A Glimpse of the Woman in First Amendment Law', Adler notes that while the U.S. Supreme Court considers live nude dancing unprotected by the First Amendment law guaranteeing free speech, it does consider that it protects pornographic films. Why, she asks, is the court so threatened by 'the live, powerful female body?' She provides the answer by reminding us that Perseus kills Medusa not while looking at her directly but while looking at her reflection on his shield, and she suggests that pornographic film provides a similar mirrored effect, 'taming' the female body by making it passive, removing its power to return the male viewer's gaze. When Perseus slays Medusa he removes the 'monstrous' threat of the woman's 'direct stare'; he 'is now free to look at her without her looking back at him'. So it is that Adler sees Perseus' shield 'as a precursor of pornographic film'. We might add that in this context, by extension, Medusa was a precursor of its victimized starlets.

VIII

Medusa as a Contemporary Icon

A dangerous attraction.
Gianni Versace

In popular culture Medusa has achieved almost rock-star status as an advertising icon and as the focus of various New Age enterprises and attitudes. The twenty-first-century Medusa is celebrated in ways that Hesiod or Homer could not have imagined, even as she retains her qualifications as a monster. The contemporary Medusa is no beautiful Romantic victim. She is perhaps closest to the femme fatale version of the Middle Ages, but more often than not it is her very monstrosity that seduces rather than any false beauty. And the contemporary witnesses of the ancient monster seem to want to be seduced by her.

Earlier interpreters used books, treatises and formal paintings to express their understandings of the Gorgon. The contemporary age continues to depict her in these traditional ways but also uses popular vehicles of information transfer such as body art and the Internet. A search for the word 'Medusa' on the Internet will turn up a scientific phenomenon called the 'Medusa Effect', described by the palaeontologist David M. Martill, in which certain fish and other animals in Brazil have been found to have undergone rapid fossilization so as to preserve even the soft matter usually absent from fossils. By continuing to follow the 'Medusa Effect' lead, the Internet surfer will find the term used in connection with the stars to make dire predictions about the future of the world. Other Medusa searches will clothe the ancient monster in pornographic images of sadomasochistic sex or will associate her with an Australian astrologer known as 'Mystic Medusa' who writes a weekly column on Facebook and apparently has a huge following.

Medusa's contemporary fame is not limited to the Internet. *The Medusa Effect* (1998) is also the title of a novel by Justin Richards involving a fictional archaeologist and the spaceship *Medusa*. Thomas Albrecht, who focuses on the image of the Medusa head as he examines images of horror in Freud, Nietzsche, Pater, Swinburne and others, uses the same title. Other writers have also made use of Medusa, including Sylvia Plath, Emilio Carballido and John Barth. Plath's poem 'Perseus: The Triumph of Wit over Suffering' (1958) sees Medusa as the perennial sufferer and Perseus as foolish man 'Armed with feathers to tickle as well as fly, / And a fun-house mirror'. In his play *Medusa* (1958) Carballido depicts Medusa as at once a force for good and evil. In his novel *Chimera* (1972) John Barth turns Medusa into an object of love for Perseus.

Perhaps the most visible contemporary depictions of Medusa are those to be found in body art. One form of upper-lip piercing is known as a Medusa piercing. There are variations involving tusk-like protrusions from the nostrils. Medusa tattoos are often more traditionally representational, with the familiar snakes-for-hair motif predominating. Medusa hair is a popular manifestation of the Medusa presence in the world of fashion and beauty products. The Medusa Salons offer a variety of Medusa hairstyles.

Films and games are also fertile ground for the celebration of Medusa power. In the film *Clash of the Titans* (1981) and its remake of 2010, the Perseus-Medusa myth is brought back to life with various non-canonical innovations. Stephen Wilk suggests that 'most people today who are aware of the story of Perseus and Medusa owe their knowledge' to the earlier film. Medusa herself, with snakes for hair and a snake-like body, remains a monster, in this case living in an Underworld temple. While alive she turns people to stone and her head continues to do so after her decapitation.

Other films featuring Medusa include *Percy Jackson & the Olympians: The Lightning Thief* (2010), based on a book of the same title by Rick Riordan (2005), in which Medusa runs a garden centre where she keeps statues of people she has turned to stone, and *The Gorgon* (1964), a Hammer Horror film in which a woman turns people to stone during the full moon. Both of these Medusas are eventually decapitated.

Medusa takes many forms in the popular game *Dungeons and Dragons*. In his 'Variant Medusas' the game author Robert Wiese describes, for example, the Changeling Medusa, the Four-legged Medusa, the Fiery Medusa and the Ghostly Medusa. All have the traditional power to turn those who look at them to stone. Medusa was the earliest of the many monsters in the game, a human/serpent combination who literally petrified others. Video games such as *Final Fantasy X*, *God of War* and *Kid Icarus* provide a stage for the Gorgon as well. The power of her head to turn people to stone and her decapitation are almost always elements of the narrative.

Medusa's name, at least, has even made its way into popular music. The Scottish singer Annie Lennox has an album called *Medusa*, containing such appropriate femme fatale titles as 'You Have Placed a Chill in my Heart'. On their album *Signing Off* (1980), the band UB40 had a song, 'Madame Medusa', that equated the Gorgon with then-prime minister Margaret Thatcher.

In all these popular culture incarnations of the Greek monster there is an element of the goth subculture that evolved from rock music in the 1980s. This was itself influenced by an earlier fascination with horror in literature and films that involved the macabre and the Other, featuring vampires, werewolves and various creative perversions of the conventional. Medusan and other outré hairstyles, piercings, extreme tattoos and black clothing are all elements of the punk/goth subculture and all would seem to reflect a need to rebel. In at least a minor way, Medusa has emerged as a symbol of that rebellion, a modern twist on the Romantic victim who in the contemporary context need not be beautiful. Again, the very attractiveness of Medusa to popular culture would seem to lie in her monstrous otherness. To the extent that sex plays a role in the adulation of Medusa it seems to be a celebration of the femme fatale, perhaps now made admirable in the context of the drive for feminine power.

Perhaps the best known contemporary use of Medusa, in this case for advertising, is that of the Italian designer Gianni Versace. There is a long history of classical figures being adopted by the advertising industry: Nike sporting equipment and Trojan condoms are two obvious examples. Versace chose the Medusa head as his logo – for haute couture, for dinner plates, for watches, for everything he

A box made by Versace featuring the fashion house's Medusa-head logo.

designed – because she had a 'certain reputation'. His choice of Medusa is clearly based on motives somewhat different from those of goths. Versace's use of Medusa is both modern and old-fashioned. His Medusa represents classical beauty, fascination and seduction. In this sense, she differs from the apotropaic Gorgoneion designs on ancient Greek pottery or shields. His Medusa head does not frighten away enemies, but is intended to immobilize her viewer for the seller's 'kill'. Just as Perseus separated Medusa's head from her body and harnessed its power to overcome enemies through petrifaction, Versace brought the Medusa head to his products to fascinate and lure his consumer 'victims'. Versace's Medusa is not the disfigured Gorgon; she is the beautiful Medusa who existed before being transformed into a monster. She is the sexual Medusa, the beautiful femme fatale. She is decadent and passionate; she possesses a fatal fascination which draws the viewer to her. As Versace put it himself when asked by the journalist Mark Seal why Medusa was his logo, 'Medusa means seduction . . . a dangerous attraction'.

With Versace, then, we reach far back to early depictions of Medusa as both dangerous and beautiful, a being capable of overcoming our common sense and redirecting our priorities. If the femme fatale Medusa of the medieval Christians was a threat to the soul, the Versace Medusa femme fatale is a symbol of a modern market-based need to feed the economy. When we gaze longingly at a Versace watch or plate, Medusa gazes out at us, luring us in, turning us to stone, as it were, for her own and her creator's purposes.

Whatever their motives, exponents of popular culture have succeeded in releasing Medusa from her monstrous Underworld life. Even more than the Romantics and psychoanalysts, they have freed her to roam in the contemporary world, turning people, Narcissus-like, into mirror images of her many incarnations.

IX

Myth as Dream

Many a man hath seen himself in dreams.
Sophocles

The first point to remember about the 'facts' of Medusa is that they are elements of a myth, and it is important to understand what is meant by this. The word 'myth' is commonly used to refer to an idea or assumed truth that is in fact untrue, or at least deeply affected by superstition. Thus it is probably a myth that George Washington never told a lie, and we can call the idea that walking under a ladder will result in bad luck a myth. The common usage of the word is derived properly enough from the more complex reality we associate with mythic narratives, stories such as those of Zeus, Herakles, Osiris, Odin, the many African and Native American tricksters and, of course, Perseus and Medusa. We know that in the compilation we call Greek mythology, Perseus, replete with magic sandals and invisibility, decapitated the Gorgon Medusa, but we know that in real life such events do not happen. We also know, however, that all religious traditions have sacred narratives that to other traditions are 'only myths'. For the African animist or the Buddhist, the stories of the parting of the Red Sea, the resurrection of Jesus and the night journey of Muhammad on his winged horse are myths, even if, for the Jew, the Christian and the Muslim the stories are vehicles for essential truth. In dealing seriously with the myths of any tradition, we would do well to remember not only that the stories are untrue in that they lie outside of our experience of reality, but that they contain information about reality as conveyed by a particular culture at a particular time, somehow articulating for the people of the culture in question a sense of the relationship between themselves and the source of existence itself. The great historian of religion Mircea Eliade saw myths in this sense as true histories that are always ultimately about reality. For example, many Native American groups say that they originally emerged from another world by way of a particular hole in the earth, sometimes located in their villages. This creation account seems obviously to be untrue: anthropologists and historians tell us that these people came to America from Central Asia. But the lives of the southwestern Native American pueblos are centred on emergence creation myths. To say that these myths are untrue is to deny the dimension from which they come and the psychological and, ultimately, material existence of the people who created them. It is to deny the people's identity. And, in any case, who are we to say that it is untrue that human beings are the products of Mother Earth?

To understand the meaning of myth more fully, it is necessary to look to its origins. The Greek word *mythos* is derived from the root sound *mu*, literally 'to make a sound with the mouth'. Originally *mythos* really meant style, and then the arrangement of words into story form. For Plato a myth was a metaphorical tale used to explain realities beyond the power of simple logic – such as the famous myth of the cave. Aristotle used *mythos* in conjunction with that most important of dramatic elements, 'plot', that which is composed of a beginning, a middle and an end, the significant arrangement of events for the ritual process that was Greek tragedy. In the Aristotelian sense *mythos* is the essence of our inherent need to articulate reality by telling stories: narratives with beginnings, middles and ends. Mythology or *mythologia* is a combination of *mythos* and *logos*, logos being the informing principle of the universe, labelled, for instance, as the 'Word' in the Christian creation story of John, which begins 'In the beginning was the Word'. To study mythology is to study myth-logic in general, or the defining myths of cultures in particular, and, finally, the cultural and collective inner life of the human quest for self-identity. That quest stretches back at least to the Palaeolithic cave paintings, themselves mythological expressions of our defining drive to make a metaphor, to 'tell a story', a drive that continues to characterize the human species as opposed to all others.

Among thinkers who take myth seriously are those who follow an essentially psychological approach. Myth scholar William Doty calls myths 'projective psyche models'. The mythologist Joseph Campbell and Carl Jung see myths as cultural dreams. For the biographer of Medusa or any other mythic character, this approach is useful. The practitioner of psychology believes that the interpretation and analysis of dreams, in spite of their obviously untrue or distorted elements, can be an important tool in the process by which an individual's psyche can be understood. In the same way, the interpretation and analysis of myths as cultural dreams can tell us much about the cultures that gave them form and perhaps about the human species itself.

At this point it is important to emphasize that myths require cultural trappings to become form, just as dreams make use of the individual's environment and particular experience to be realized. If we study the myths of the Native American Hopi tribe we will inevitably note the emphasis on the people's original emergence from a particular hole in the earth and on mysterious spirit figures called *kachinas*. We will also come across a character known as Spider Woman. The first job of an interpreter and analyst of these myths would be to attempt to understand what the emergence from earth, the *kachinas* and Spider Woman reveal about the collective psyche of the Hopi as opposed to other peoples. Other cultures, after all, believe they were created *ex nihilo* by some supreme deity, or that particular gods have many avatars or incarnations, or that certain tricksters brought evil into the world, or that a god created the world and then left it alone. All such elements of particular cultural mythologies – Greek, Egyptian, Christian, African animistic – potentially can reveal to the analyst something of the inner nature of the cultures in question. The ancient Egyptian fascination with the death and renewal of the god-king Osiris can be related to the annual flooding of the Nile. The escape of creator gods and the strong influence of tricksters in African myths must be studied in relation to African views of the precarious nature of life.

It is here that the analyst of myths must take a leap. Questions must be asked. If I do not happen to be an anthropologist concerned with Hopi culture, for example, why do the emergence creation story and Spider Woman speak to me so deeply? Why am I moved by these strange elements of Hopi myth? How do Egyptian dying gods or African animist disappearing ones speak to me through the barrier between my culture and cultures that are foreign, and perhaps even uninteresting to me?

One answer to these questions is suggested by thinkers such as Eliade, Campbell and Jung, who see universal elements in myths that are embedded in the human psyche as a whole, what Jung called our 'collective unconscious'. By comparing myths from various cultures they see the emergence of archetypes, the universal symbols that transcend cultures even as they require cultural 'clothes' to come to life. In his famous analysis *The Hero with a Thousand Faces* (1949), for instance, Joseph Campbell revealed, through the comparison of mythic hero myths, a universal or archetypal hero's life story, a 'monomyth' which exists in shadow form behind all of the particular cultural dreams of heroes. Quetzalcoatl is definitely a product of Meso-American culture. But his miraculous conception by way of a virgin mother and the breath of the high god relates him firmly to other heroes who enter the world through miraculous conceptions. Buddha, Jesus, King Arthur, Horus and Superman are a few of many such heroes. The universal hero's life is a quest – for the Holy Grail, for the Golden Fleece, for the kingdom of God, for a lost father. The Underworld to which Herakles descends as a part of his life's quest is a Greek Underworld populated by other Greeks and reflecting a Greek sense of life after death. But Herakles is only one of many heroes who in their own cultural clothes descend to the Underworld. The Sumerian hero Gilgamesh, the Japanese Izanagi and Izanami, the Norse Hermóðr, Jesus, the Mesopotamian Inanna and many others also descend. The hero pattern involves many elements. The hero is often hidden as a child from forces that would destroy him. He often serves as a scapegoat and even dies. He nearly always returns from his experience with death. Jung and Campbell consider the world hero with his many faces and analyse him psychologically, seeing in the hero's life a metaphor for the human psyche on a journey that is universal even as, again, it requires cultural trappings to be realized. Universal archetypal elements allow us to break through cultural barriers, and draw us into myths and fascinate us.

Archetypes are not limited to the hero journey. An analysis of any cultural dream can reveal various elements that belong to us all rather than to any one particular culture. When we analyse dreams we look for items that somehow stand out, recurrent themes or seemingly irrelevant elements that strike us as being logically out of place yet somehow important. The same is true of the analysis of the cultural dreams we call myths. To understand the meaning of a cultural dream we must be aware of both patterns and unusual elements. We can then, partly by way of comparison with other cultural dreams, consider these patterns and unusual elements not only as cultural factors but as culture-transcending archetypes that have relevance for us today. Several motifs that stand out in the Medusa myth can serve as examples of these culture-transcending archetypal themes, touchstones that demand the attention of the interpreter of the Medusa dream. These include, for instance, triplets, snakes, female monsters, decapitation, sacrifice, and the centrality of eyes and seeing.

Triplets

The reader of the Medusa myth cannot help but be struck by the presence of triplets. Most notably, there are three Graiae and three Gorgons. The number three, of course, has significance in all cultures and in archaic and classical Greece, as in other Indo-European cultures, the number was often associated with goddesses – specifically the so-called Triple Goddess. In fact, thinkers as varied as Jane Harrison, Marija Gimbutas and Carl Jung see the triple goddess as an essential element of human culture in its earliest forms. Jung and his colleagues Karoli Kerenyi and Eric Neumann see the number three as a number associated with ancient earth-based chthonic goddess rites. Various goddess triads in later cultures reflect this ancient tendency or archetype. In India the wives of the great triad of gods, Brahma, Vishnu and Shiva, themselves form a triad of Sarasvati, Lakshmi and Parvati, the three goddesses being aspects of the Great Goddess, or Devi, who is the nurturing Parvati as well as her somewhat monstrous counterparts, the deathly Kali and the ferocious Durga. In Ireland aspects of the triple goddess appear in the personifications of Ireland, Ériu, Banba and Fódla, as well as in the great goddess Morrígan who forms a triad with Badb and Macha, representing warfare and power as well as fertility.

But it must be emphasized that as representatives of the triple goddess, the Graiae and the Gorgons are figures pushed to the margins of reality, confined to faraway lands and plagued by an essential monstrosity that approaches the ridiculous. The Graiae have one eye and one tooth between them; the Gorgons are surrounded by the debris of their victims, and their faces are ugly and frightening in the extreme. If they are the triple goddess, they are greatly diminished by the patriarchal culture that tells their story. Such ancient matriarchal constructs as the triple goddess are of course anathaema to the Olympian-oriented creators of the classical Medusa dream.

Snakes

Medusa has snakes rather than hair springing from her head, as do her sisters in some variations of the story. The association of the Gorgons with snakes suggests another earlier vision of feminine

The Minoan 'snake goddess', *c.* 1600 BCE, faience.

power. Barbara Walker, author of *The Woman's Encyclopedia of Myths and Secrets* (1983), argues that 'a female face surrounded by serpent hair was an ancient, widely recognized symbol of divine female wisdom.' In ancient Libya a Medusa figure was one of a set of triplet sisters who personified wisdom. Snakes were associated with these sisters because snakes also represented wisdom. Depictions of a great goddess of Crete dating from about 1600 BCE show the goddess holding up snakes in each hand.

In ancient Egypt Wadjet was a snake-headed goddess who later became Bast, the fierce goddess whose eye is the eye of Horus and the eye of the great sun god, Ra. Eyes and snakes are, of course, both basic to the Medusa myth. In an early Pelasgian creation myth, Eurynome, a Gaia figure, first created the serpent Ophion, who participated in the process of the world's birth. Coatlicue, the mother of the Meso-American god-king Quetzalcoatl, was served by snakes. Before snakes obtained a bad name – in the Genesis myth, for instance – they appear to have represented regeneration, healing and fertility in what some might call a phallic association with goddess figures. But again, an element that had once been a symbol of the power of the earth-based feminine becomes in the Medusa myth of the classical period an absurd depiction of the perversion of that power. The positive serpent of the ancient goddess becomes the grotesque substitute for a monster's hair.

Female Monsters

Monstrosity and femaleness are basic to the Graiae and especially the Gorgons with their tusks, snake-infested hair, staring eyes and protruding tongues. That the confluence of monstrosity and femaleness is at least in part a peculiarly Greek cultural element is suggested by the fact that by the Roman period Medusa had regained some of her beauty and become as much a victim as a force that must be destroyed. The confluence of monstrosity and femaleness suggests a fear of female power and an anti-female message in the Greek myth and Greek culture. The same confluence also seems to be important in a somewhat larger, more archetypal context in which heroes slay female monsters representing an earlier power. Greek mythology has other slayers of female monsters. Bellerophon kills the Chimera; Apollo kills the Delphic Python. Monster-slayers are endemic to world mythology and, as in the case of the Greek examples, they usually represent the destruction of an old order in favour of a new one. The Chimera represents the old chthonic period that must be overcome by the new hero with new values. Apollo's defeat of the python represents the use of Olympian reason to overcome the earth-based powers of primordial chaos.

The killing of a female figure of the ancient Gaian sea-monster heritage by a shining hero of the new Olympian order has an almost obvious parallel and possibly a source in the Mesopotamian myth of the slaying of the primordial female monster Tiamat by the Babylonian city god and patriarchal hero Marduk. The Medusa–Perseus conflict, then, as we have seen, may reflect a struggle between conflicting world views, a struggle in which an ancient feminine power is destroyed and replaced by a new masculine one. The reworkings of the Perseus-Medusa story by rationalists like Palaephatus, Diodorus and Pausanias speak directly to this struggle, emphasizing once and for all that Perseus, representing a patriarchal force, put an end to archaic rulership by women.

The Eye

A particular oddity in the Medusa myth is the eye shared by the three Graiae. The Graiae tooth stands out too but seems to have been quickly dropped as an issue by mythmakers. If nothing else, the tooth seems to emphasize the unity and mutual dependency of the triplets in question. The eye, however, which Perseus takes from the Graiae, is the necessary key to his gaining the information he needs to proceed on his journey. As we have seen, in the quasi-historical version of the Perseus-Medusa story told by the sceptical Athenean Palaephatus, the Eye was a person in the employ of Medusa and her sisters who was captured by Perseus and used as a hostage in the hero's attempt to obtain a statue of Athene. In our mythic tale, the eye seems to point to other eyes, those soon to be dealt with by Perseus in the deadly stare of the Medusa herself. The mythic eye is a much more powerful and universal object than the one 'explained' by Palaephatus. It is the Medusa stare that Perseus must avoid, but which he can use effectively against his enemies.

Most cultures will recognize in the deadly stare of Medusa the tradition of the evil eye. According to believers, certain people possess the power in their eyes to inflict injury, bad luck or other evil on those towards whom their stare is directed. Images of that stare may be used as protective talismans, as in the case of the Gorgon heads, the Gorgoneia discussed earlier. Often talismans against the evil eye take the form of what in parts of the Middle East are called nazars, little beads composed of blue and white and sometimes images of an eye. The hamsa, the image of a hand with an eye image in its palm, is also common as a talisman. In Jewish culture the hand may be called the Hand of Miriam; in Islamic culture the Hand of Fatima. Scholars generally believe that the evil eye concept arose from a universal dislike of being stared at. People do not like being 'stared

A nazar amulet, for protection against the evil eye.

A hamsa hand, believed to provide protection from the evil eye.

down'. Certain looks elicit certain sayings: 'If looks could kill' is a good example, one particularly applicable to Medusa.

Sacrifice

In Greek culture, Medusa is clearly a victim, a being long detached from any archetypal role as a reigning queen or goddess. This is established by the story of her being raped by Poseidon: the new god of the sea rapes the daughter of the old god of the sea, the goddess of wisdom punishes her, and Perseus kills the rape victim. On the surface, one of the most curious aspects of Medusa is the fact that unlike her parents and her sisters, she is mortal. A simple way of explaining this oddity is just to note that within the myth/dream world there is an inner consistency of reality that owes more to narrative need than to reason. Medusa is mortal because Perseus must kill her. To put it another way, Medusa is a scapegoat, a ritualistic victim set up by the Olympians to represent an old order that must be eliminated. By stripping her of immortality, the mythmakers in effect lay the

Gorgon on the sacrificial altar so that Perseus can do what he has to do. The ritualistic elements here are many: the special cap from Hades, the *kibisis*, the winged sandals, Athena's mirror, the special adamantine sickle from Hermes. Athena even guides Perseus' hand as he slices off Medusa's head. Once again, Medusa seems clearly to be a sacrificial victim in a cultural war waged by the patriarchal Olympian culture against the old Gaian one. The cap, the *kibisis*, the sandals, the mirror and the sickle are the new magic used against the old chthonic magic and power of the Gaian gods. We can imagine, as scholars such as Robert Graves and Marija Gimbutas have, that such a struggle existed in actual fact in pre-archaic Greece and that clearly the Olympians won.

Decapitation

Perseus decapitated Medusa with Athene's help, using the adamantine sickle provided by Hermes. The decapitation motif is a prominent one in world mythology. Gilgamesh decapitates Humbaba, David does the same to Goliath, and Gawain decapitates the Green Knight. In almost every case a hero representing a new order separates the head from what is seen as a monstrous being from an older order. The fact that decapitation rather than a stab to the heart or some other means of execution is chosen by the hero is what demands our analytic attention.

There have been many attempts to explain the significance of the decapitation archetype. As discussed earlier, Sigmund Freud saw in the act of decapitation a symbol of castration. The serpents that were Medusa's hair, for instance, suggested penises to Freud. 'A multiplication of penis symbols signifies castration', he wrote. Others – Richard Payne Knight and Klaus Theweleit, for example – have seen in the decapitation a male reaction to a fear of female potency.

It is possible that the decapitation in the Medusa myth has a more cultural and more direct explanation, albeit in the context of the larger archetypal theme of the sacrificial or scapegoat victim. The reason for decapitation here is very possibly simply to detach the still powerful head. Freed from the body of the Gorgon, the Medusa head could become the primary weapon of the hero Perseus and

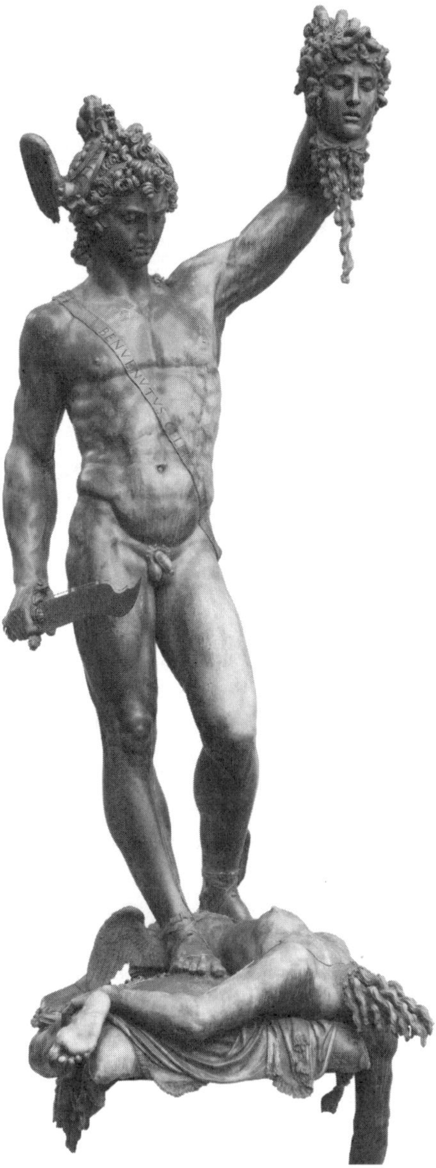

Benvenuto Cellini, *Perseus with the Head of Medusa*, 1554, bronze.

eventually the apotropaic talisman that supposedly protected people in Greek society from other kinds of evil. In short, the dominance of the head in the overall myth is reinforced by decapitation, and decapitation 'explains' the existence of the Gorgoneion.

Conclusion: Who is Medusa?

It has always been the prime function of mythology and rite to supply the symbols that carry the human spirit forward.
Joseph Campbell

When facing the ubiquitous presence of Medusa as envisioned and interpreted by different cultures and individuals in so many ways over the centuries, the historian is still left with the essential question: who is this strange, even obscure, mythological character, who is like nothing ever seen in the world but has remained embedded in the collective human psyche since she came into being some time in pre-history?

In her essay 'Transforming Medusa', Charlotte Currie suggests that all the transformations of the original mythic Medusa – including the earliest ones – are more reflections of the transformers than of Medusa herself. Medusa, she says, has 'simply become a mirror for subsequent interpreters, and we have become either her slayer or the dread Gorgon herself'.

The Medusa life story as told by classical authors from Homer to Ovid is clear enough. Psychological and archetypal analogues in other parts of the world are just as clear. Medusa's life and persona have been variously interpreted by analysts from the classical, Renaissance, medieval, Romantic, realist, modern and contemporary periods, and the biographer is left with many views of this mysterious being who has never lost her power to fascinate. Depending on the witnesses, she is figured variously as a hideous monster, a femme fatale, a beautiful victim, a psychological and aesthetic symbol, a feminist heroine and a commercial icon. Over the centuries, Medusa has been revealed in so many personae, many of which contradict each other, that she leaves us with a dilemma. How can our subject be so many beings at once?

The obvious place to begin an evaluation of these interpretations is the classical myth, at least a part of which was acknowledged as early as the eighth century BCE by Homer and Hesiod and later by many other poets and historians in ancient Greece and Rome. It was retold in some detail, especially by Apollodorus and Ovid. Although the details of the retellings vary, there is an essential consistency in the classical period that justifies our calling the classical myth canonical, just as we call the Book of Genesis canonical, despite its having been written by at least two authors who disagree on such details as the creation of Eve: was she created with Adam, as Genesis 1 has it, or from one of Adam's ribs, as we are told in Genesis 2? In the same way, the four gospels of the New Testament are accepted as the canonical life of Jesus in spite of inconsistencies in their details.

The canonical myth of Medusa, which exists in conjunction with the myth of Perseus, whatever the views and priorities of its interpreters over the ages, has certain necessary elements. The myth makes no sense unless we accept the fact that, for whatever reason, the once beautiful Medusa is a much-feared hideous monster with snakes for hair, the mere sight of whom turns men to stone. A strangely mortal offspring of the pre-classical Gaian generation of monstrous immortals, Medusa owes her unfortunate situation to the enmity of the Olympian gods, especially Athene, the virgin warrior goddess, whose hatred of Medusa has to do with what the goddess sees as sexual misconduct. With the help of Athene and Hermes, the hero Perseus, miraculously fathered by Zeus, vows to kill Medusa. By using Athene's shield as a mirror, he avoids looking at Medusa, and, with the goddess's direct assistance and several magical objects procured after overpowering Medusa's relatives the Graiae triplets, he decapitates her. He then escapes from Medusa's two Gorgon sisters and eventually lives 'happily ever after' with his wife Andromeda, having first used the head of Medusa to turn his enemies to stone.

Of all of these elements, the one truly necessary one, without which the myth is meaningless, is the fact that Medusa is a monster; that she represents a well-known mythological category. Her mythological 'sisters' in Greece are such figures as the Chimera and the Hydra. Each of these monsters belongs to a family of gods that precedes the ruling divine family. Each is destroyed by a hero who represents the new ruling family.

The Chimera is perhaps the monster most easily compared to Medusa. Like the Gorgon, the Chimera was known to both Homer and Hesiod. Homer describes her as a fire-breathing monster who was part lion, part goat and part snake. She is a close relative of Medusa. Her mother was Echidna, who like the Gorgons and the Graiae was born of Keto by Phorkys. All were grandchildren of the ancient earth goddess Gaia. Echidna was half beautiful woman and half serpent. The 'Mother of Monsters', she ate humans raw. Together with the half-man, half-dragon 'Father of Monsters', Gaia's son Typhon, who nearly defeated Zeus in the war in heaven, she produced, among other horrors, the Chimera; the Hydra, a multi-headed water serpent; and the double-headed Orthus, who with his own mother produced the Sphinx and others. All these monsters, then, were of the old Gaian order and all had at least partial serpent ancestry. And, most importantly, a great many of them served the ancient Greek mythologists as appropriate targets for the feats of Olympian-backed heroes. Zeus' son Herakles destroyed the Hydra. The Chimera became the victim of Bellerophon, who flew to battle on the back of Medusa's son by Poseidon, the winged horse Pegasus.

In an earlier example of a monster killing from Mesopotamia, the Babylonian creation myth the *Enuma Elish* tells how the female monster Tiamat, the personification of the sea, gave birth to the first generation of gods, but was eventually killed by Marduk, the city god of Babylon. Marduk was now to be the leader of a new divine order that was opposed to the primordial chaos now associated with Tiamat.

In all these myths of the monster killed by heroes, it seems clear that the monsters represented primordial chaos to the religious systems current at the time of the development of the myths in question. That the monsters are often female suggests, as noted earlier, the upsurge of patriarchy over what was perhaps a more feminine-based culture. But more importantly, it suggests a male sense that feminine strength was serpent-like: mysterious, death-related and dangerous. In Greece it was centred in Gaia, the dark depths of the earth, as opposed to in Zeus, the sky king of heavenly Olympus who, together with such figures as Apollo and Athene, represented order and reason in spite of his philandering and eccentricities. It was up to a human type known as the hero – a type closely related to the Olympians – to impose Olympian order on the chaos of the Gaian monsters. Sir James Frazer in *The Golden Bough* (1922) and Robert Graves in *The White Goddess* (1948) suggest that the female monsters with their serpent characteristics might represent the destructive side of the Great Goddess of the ancient fertility cults. N. Douglas, in an essay on the ultimate serpent form known as dragons, speaks of the dragon as 'the personification of life within the earth . . . which, being unknown and uncontrollable, is *ipso facto* hostile to man'.

An element that stands out in the Medusa myth, and makes it somewhat different from and better known than the other female monster myths, is the concept of the transference of monster power: from evil, at the ends of the earth, to good, in the world bathed in the Olympian sun. Whatever the details of this canonical myth, it is clear that the essence of its earliest incarnations centred on the Medusa head in the form of Gorgoneia, following in traditions such as the apotropaic heads of Bes and Humbaba, which were already well established in Egypt and Mesopotamia. Homer speaks of the head as 'a thing of fear and horror', and the Gorgoneia on early temples and amulets served as frightening defence talismans against dark forces such as the evil eye. Perseus used the head to defeat enemies. Athena and Zeus himself carried Gorgoneia on their battle equipment. The crucial point here is that what the Greeks considered to be evil itself – the monstrous other – is transformed into an object of protection, a point that will be central to a final understanding of Medusa.

Perseus himself, as a bona fide hero, is, like Medusa, a representative of a category well recognized by the Greeks and other cultures. We recognize the hero archetype in Perseus because, like Jesus, Herakles, Horus and so many others of the type, he is conceived miraculously by way of a divine agent. We recognize him because, like Sigurd, Moses, Horus and others, he is hidden as a child from evil forces who would otherwise destroy him. Most of all, we recognize him because, like all true heroes, he undertakes a seemingly impossible quest.

It is of course difficult to see a whole picture if one is in the picture. The ancient Greeks did not compare Perseus to Moses or Horus, and they did not compare Medusa to the older Mesopotamian Tiamat. As far as they were concerned, Perseus and Medusa belonged exclusively to them and acted out a ritual sacrifice in which masculine power appropriately defeated female power; in which the forces of Zeus defeated those of an earlier earth-based religion and turned the latter's evil power into a power for good. Perseus represented good; Medusa represented evil.

The ritual sacrifice idea becomes clear as soon as Perseus announces his intention to obtain the head of Medusa. This announcement immediately establishes the importance of the Medusa head and begins the process by which the myth will 'explain' the existence of the popular Gorgoneion. There is, after all, no good reason for Perseus to announce such an intention. Polydektes does not challenge him to find the head. And realistically, the quest is essentially impossible, because of the well-known power of the Medusan gaze and Perseus' lack of sufficient weaponry. In the dream world of myth, however, such obstacles can be overcome. Perseus boasts of his impossible intention because he is a hero: because, as the son of God, he has been chosen as Herakles, Bellerophon, Jesus, Moses and Horus are chosen. The necessary weapons will be provided by the Olympians: the sandals, the cap, the *kibisis*, the sickle, the mirror-shield – all elements of the ritual. And the hero's alter ego, Athene, will guide his arm in the sacred act of decapitation. The fact that Medusa alone, of all the children of Keto and Phorkys, was mortal makes no sense in anything but a mythic context. She is mortal because the sacrificial ritual demands that she be killed and the ritual here is more important than mere facts. Without the decapitation there can be no Gorgoneion. In the same way, the Greeks would not have thought less of Perseus for being helped so significantly by Athene any more than they would have thought less of Odysseus for having been helped by her. Athene was the goddess of wisdom, and wisdom plays a necessary and appropriate role in the achievement of Perseus' – and perhaps anyone's – quest. The fact that Athene is, in every sense, *with* him decisively marks Perseus as a true hero of the culture.

For those standing outside the picture looking in, other elements come to the surface. Characters and events seen outside of the context of the original myth become less ritualistic, more reflective of the interests and perspectives of the cultures viewing them. It can be argued that explanations of the Medusa story from the Middle Ages to the present day are merely aspects of the continuing expansion of the myth itself, just as the myth developed from Homer to Ovid. The myth continues to grow as the human mind reflects on it. On the other hand, as noted earlier, it can also be argued that a specific myth did emerge in a final canonical form from the Graeco-Roman or classical period, and that later explanations of or adaptations of that myth are distortions created in the interest of particular priorities and ideologies.

The idea that Medusa represents the dangerous erotic power of women is a consistent element in the allegorical treatment of the Gorgon during the Middle Ages and Renaissance. Lucan compares that power to the seductive dressing of Roman women. Lucian suggests that Medusa turns men to stone not with her stare but with her dangerous female beauty. Fulgentius and Leone Ebreo see Medusa as a metaphor for the power that women have over the minds of men. For the poets of the *Roman de la rose*, for Dante, for Petrarch and for Natale Conti, Medusa represents the erotic power of women over men's souls. In short, by the medieval period Medusa had become a femme fatale. Our question must be whether this attribution is a valid continuation of the canonical story or a perversion of it.

In one sense it can be said to be a natural extension of the original story. It seems evident that the original myth expressed patriarchal attitudes of the Greeks towards women. Medusa was dangerous and she was female. There is also the fact that she is said to have once compared her own beauty favourably to that of Athene. When we meet the Gorgon in the myth, however, she is clearly a monster. There is no sense that it is her beauty or erotic power being dangerous to men – either to their minds or souls. All men have to fear is her stare, which will turn them into stone. In short, Medusa in the Greek myth is an appropriate target for the archetypal monster-slayer, a role played by Perseus, who is in no way tempted by Medusan charms. In the archetypal sense it makes little difference even that Medusa is female. Heroes like Perseus and his relative Herakles kill monsters, not necessarily female monsters. They kill the remnants of an ancient chaos that threatens the order established by their divine fathers. In this sense John Harrington's interpretation of Perseus as godliness (he is the son of God) allied with reason (Athene) comes close to a truth expressed in the Greek myth.

This aside, however, the evolution of Medusa as a femme fatale would seem to be a substitution of a medieval and Renaissance Christian archetype for a Greek one. Christianity's association of sexuality, women and sin – a new kind of monstrosity – is made emblematic in the femme fatale. But Medusa in the myth itself is not a femme fatale, and making her one would seem to be a distortion to fit the Christian theology and ideology prevalent during the period in question. Femmes fatales threaten men – including heroes – with their sexually seductive powers. Medusa does not pose a sexual threat to Perseus. On the contrary, she is an ugly monster to be destroyed.

In the Romantic and Victorian approach to Medusa the understanding of the Gorgon changes once again to meet new intellectual fashions. Shelley, in his unfinished poem on the Medusa painting wrongly attributed to Leonardo, sees not the justifiable decapitation of evil but the 'tempestuous loveliness of terror' reflected on the severed head. Rossetti sees beauty in the Medusa head. For the Romantics the ultimate beauty was that which emerged from the juxtaposition of pleasure and pain, and is particularly evident in the beautiful victim of the establishment. In this context, Perseus is the instrument of the repressive religious and political status quo and Medusa becomes the hero. The fact that she had once defied Athene by comparing her beauty favourably to the goddess's only confirms her position as a glorious rebel against arbitrary authority. The fact that she was raped by Poseidon, and punished for it by Athene, both representatives of that authority, serves to make her a victim and makes her sympathetic to those who condemn the tendency of traditional societies to punish the victim of rape rather than the rapist. It is the rape and subsequent punishment of the rape victim that makes the Romantic and Victorian views of Medusa particularly attractive to modern students of the myth.

Unfortunately, however, the Medusa of the myth, although admittedly victimized in the past, has nevertheless become a terrifying monster with overwhelming powers of destruction. Quite simply, Shelley and Rossetti 'Romanticize' her. Ironically, she has managed to *médusé* them to such an extent that they see someone who is not there. In so doing they undermine our understanding of the positive role of Perseus in the myth.

In the post-Victorian age of realism, Medusa was adopted as a somewhat bloodless symbol into the political, philosophical and historical theories of Nietzsche and Marx; the anthropological and religious ideas of Jane Harrison and Marija Gimbutas, and the existentialism of Jean-Paul Sartre. The problem with most of these approaches is that the Medusa of the myth is co-opted by theories to which she is forced to adapt with little concern for her actual life story.

In the same period the psychological approaches to the myth became particularly popular. But today Freud's association of Medusa's decapitation with castration anxiety in connection with a child's view of his mother's genitals seems far-fetched and even comic in the aftermath of a century of psychological – particularly Freudian – dominance. And even if we were to accept the castration interpretation, we would have no better idea of who Medusa actually is. In short, Freud simply uses an aspect of Medusa's story to illustrate a theory. He has no particular interest in Medusa herself.

The Jungian psychological approach is more useful to the biographer. It centres on the real nature of Medusa as an archetypal representative of the chaotic side of female personality, of which Athene represents the opposite. For Jung, characters in myth are embodiments of universal psychic tendencies present in the 'collective unconscious'. Medusa is an archetype of the collective unconscious and so is Athene. As a version of the hero archetype, Perseus would represent the drive of the individual for self-realization or individuation. The approach, as it applies to Athene and Medusa, touches on the interesting point of a deep, even mirroring, relationship between the two, but it seems too sexist for our day, smacking of the now-discredited hysteria argument once popular in connection with illnesses and women.

The postmodernist French attempt to add to and even to rewrite the Gorgon myth is a valid enough approach, if we believe that the myth is a living reality with the capacity to absorb new details. But in this case, the theorists actually change well-established elements of Medusa's life as recorded in the canonical texts. Once again the events of Medusa's life take a minor second place to sometimes obfuscating theories and concepts. Although what Derrida says about Hegel and Judaism is interesting enough, he uses Medusa as an illustration of his theory. He has no interest in shedding light on the Gorgon herself. The same can be said of the addition by Marin and Caillois (and also by the North Americans Siebers and Hiebert) of the idea that Medusa is herself *médusé* by looking at her own reflection.

Among today's intellectuals the feminist interpretation of Medusa is the most popular. This approach is inevitable since Medusa is, in the canonical myth, a female victim of a male figure backed up by a patriarchal religious system in which goddesses are either vamps or masculinized hunters and warriors. Following the lead of Hélène Cixous, Sarah Kofman, Teresa de Lauretis, Stephen Heath, Susan Bowers, Patricia Klindienst and Amy Adler all see in the Perseus-Medusa myth a phallocentric story in which the female is objectified and turned into a monster by the male, who essentially fears her sexual power. The feminist argument is strong and difficult to refute. The patriarchal hero – the son of the patriarch – kills the female monster of the old feminine order. The myth does make sense as an 'explanation' of or description of what might be called universal sexism. Cixous suggests that women need to look straight at the Medusa to discover her beauty and the beauty of their own bodies and sexuality.

But once again, as in the case of the medieval, Renaissance, Romantic and postmodernist discussions of Medusa, we are faced with the problem of the existing myth. As Charlotte Currie suggests, every age has rewritten the myth to fit its own needs. The feminist myth, however timely, is not the myth told by the Greeks. What the feminist approach ignores is the central element of the myth, the fact that Medusa, however unfairly created as such, is a hideous monster. Cixous, like Dante, Shelley, Freud, Derrida and so many others, has used the myth to speak to contemporaneous beliefs and concerns but in so doing has distorted the original story – the canonical myth.

The same can be said of the contemporary use of Medusa in popular culture. The monstrous qualities of the Gorgon become 'cool' in tattoos and hair styles. Her supposedly seductive qualities are useful in the selling of haute couture and erotica. But once again, the contemporary renderings seem faddish and peripheral to the real meaning of the myth except in so far as an aspect of the myth speaks to a tendency towards narcissism in the human psyche.

However tempting the rewritings of the myth may be, the biographer of Medusa must finally determine not only the identity of this being as she exists in the actual myth but what she has to do with human identity, regardless of cultural practices, intellectual and popular movements and changing points of view.

To begin a final interpretation of the Medusa story, we would do well to return to the assumption that myth can be compared to dreams and to a further assumption that whether a given narrative to be interpreted is a cultural or personal dream – a myth or a sleeping narrative – it must be recognized from the beginning that the characters and events in the dream belong to the dreamer. Distortions of reality that mark these phenomena are not so much external intrusions as reflections of something in the memory or unconscious of the dreamer. Myths and dreams act out in narrative form concerns, conflicts, fears and challenges within the culture or the individual dreamer. The myth of Medusa as a Greek cultural dream reflects, as we have seen, questions that concerned the collective Greek psyche – questions having to do with male–female status and power, with the importance of the number three, with the evil-eye power of the Gorgoneion, with traditions of sacrifice, decapitation and the relationship between divinity and humans, represented by gods and heroes. In the Medusa myth, Perseus, Athene, Hermes, the Graiae, Andromeda, Danaë and Medusa herself are all aspects of the same collective personality. For the story to be fully told, the characters all need each other. One indication of this need, for example, is the fact that Perseus and Athene cooperate in the killing of Medusa. In the 'real' world outside of dream we might well ask why, if Athene hates Medusa so much, she does not simply kill her herself? Why involve the complex elements associated with Perseus and his role? Why involve a human hero?

Again, feminists and others are right, of course, to disapprove of the vision of reality and the priorities expressed in this myth. To the modern world it is sexist and brutal. But our views do not change the reality of the myth. We are not the Greeks, and it is an ancient Greek myth.

But why, then, is the myth of Medusa so fascinating to modern readers? What do we care about a patriarchal hero, conceived by a god in a shower of gold, killing an ancient monster and marrying a victimized maiden? Medieval and Renaissance Christian scholars used the myth to develop metaphors in support of their point of view. The Romantics latched on to Medusa as a beautiful victim, a symbol of Romanticism itself. Freud and his followers attributed the interest in the myth to fears of castration. Sartre and other intellectuals have focused on the universal confrontation with the Other. Whatever form the post-classical interpretations of Medusa take, they reveal an enduring fascination with her.

To explain that universal and seemingly eternal fascination, an approach that emphasizes common motifs and archetypal constructs would seem to be the most promising. There are elements in the Medusa myth that strike chords in us even though we are not ancient Greeks. They do this because they respond to universal human concerns. The cultural dream thus becomes a universal dream. The events in the myth correspond to events in our collective inner lives. They become what James Hillman would call 'the psyche itself in its imaginative visibility'. And in this context, too, it must be stressed that in the universal dream, all the characters and events are aspects of the same collective personality; they are all aspects of us. Again, the characters and events all need each other.

It is fair to suggest that Medusa is, first of all, one of many representatives in world mythology of the Other that must be confronted. She shares with the likes of the Chimera, St George's dragon, Marduk's Tiamat and so many other victims of heroic slaughter the fact that she is above all a monster. In terms of the universal, as opposed to the particular cultural dream of the Greeks, it really makes no difference whether Medusa is male or female. True, from the Greek cultural standpoint it seems likely that she represents the threat of an older female, magic and earth-based culture that the archaic Greeks, the Babylonians and others were replacing with a male-dominated patriarchal system centred on the gods above rather than the goddesses below. But Medusa's possible antecedents in Mesopotamia and Egypt were sometimes male, sometimes female. Even in Greece there are depictions of Medusa that are male. Again, what finally matters to us, in spite of the various post-classical interpretations we have traced, is the fact that Medusa is a monster. It is her monstrous appearance and above all the fact that she turns people into stone that captures our attention.

But the biographer must ask here why Medusa has been so much more a presence in human consciousness than equally monstrous creatures such as the Chimera or even the Sphinx. The answer is in part provided by the various approaches to Medusa over the centuries. The medieval and Renaissance Christians feared her because she was seen as a sexual being and therefore as a different kind of threat from other monsters. Freud, too, recognized her sexuality. She had, after all, had sexual attraction for Poseidon. The Romantics pitied her and feminists have celebrated her because she was a victim, even a once beautiful victim. And the Greeks themselves differentiated her even from her sisters, because unlike them she was mortal. Medusa attracts our attention, in short, not only because of her hideous deformities, but also because as a mortal, as a sexual being and as a victim, she was human: one of us.

One way to consider our attachment to Medusa is to construct a psychological model. In this model Medusa, as a monster, is that aspect within us that immobilizes us psychologically. She is the demon within, our shadow, our eternal demon, the 'dark side' of our lives that we cannot bear to look at directly. In the film epic *Star Wars*, she is Darth Vader, the dark side of the Force, the negative side of reality that must be confronted by the hero Luke Skywalker before he can realize his potential. She is the ubiquitous dragon who must be destroyed. We must confront her and in so doing overcome her, if we are to be psychologically whole. Left un-confronted, Medusa eats away at our well-being.

In specific terms, the demon might be alcoholism, sexual addiction or some obsession. The possibilities are endless. The inner demon represented by Medusa is powerful and immobilizing. Humans are fascinated by Medusa in all her cultural incarnations and always have been because we recognize her as a familiar, as a power that challenges us with her gaze.

But she is more than that. The persona of the collective dream is drawn to the monster not only as a natural enemy which must be destroyed, but as a source of productive power when controlled. The persona in the Medusa dream is represented by Perseus. As we have seen, Perseus appears on the scene as a recognizable hero, apparently a son of Zeus. It is his miraculous conception or virgin birth that immediately signals the beginning of the heroic 'monomyth'. The hero enters the world of humanity through the only possible door – a human mother – but he belongs finally to no parents; he belongs to us all. In a sense he *is* us all, or at least our representative on the quest that will follow. The shower of gold through which the king of gods implanted his seed in Danaë signifies a particularly royal conception, the conception of a true hero who comes into the world for a reason. Comparable grandeur is found in the conception of the Buddha by way of a white elephant in Queen Maha Maya's dream, or the descent of the Holy Spirit upon the humble Virgin Mary or the breath of God that led to the conception of the Mesoamerican hero Quetzalcoatl.

The next step in the monomythic life of the archetypal hero is the resistance he faces from the representatives of the status quo, those who would deny the new energy, the threat to themselves, they see in the child hero. There are always forces that tend to undermine our spiritual and emotional growth and it is always necessary to confront these forces. Moses is hidden from Pharaoh in the bullrushes; Sigurd escapes King Sigmund by being hidden in a glass vessel that floats down the river; Jesus is protected from Herod by being taken into Egypt. In the case of Perseus it is his own grandfather who plays the role of the wicked king. His disruptive nature is confirmed not only in his treatment of his daughter Danaë but also by the information we are given that he had fought with his twin brother in his mother's womb, relating him archetypally to other feuding brothers such as Cain and Abel in the Bible or Set and Osiris in Egyptian mythology. Perseus and his mother are separated from the king in a basket-like vessel which is thrown into the sea.

Frequently in the monomyth the divine child – the young hero – is recovered by or delivered to an ordinary rather than a noble individual, a shepherd or a fisherman, for instance. Oedipus is found by a shepherd, Sigurd by the blacksmith Mimir. Perseus is received by the fisherman Diktys. The importance of ordinary people here is that they, as opposed to kings and heroes, represent us all.

In the case of Perseus, he is given over as a child to Diktys' brother, another wicked king, Polydektes. It is through the very wickedness and enmity of this king that Perseus discovers his particular quest, his self-realizing path to herohood or wholeness. Like Herakles, he maintains that he can accomplish the impossible. He will obtain the much-feared head of the Gorgon Medusa, and immediately he leaves on the necessary heroic quest. On this quest he is aided specifically by the goddess of wisdom, Athene, and a god of magic and deep penetrating knowledge, Hermes. The message here is that wisdom and knowledge are necessary qualities for the accomplishing of the impossible, the attainment of self-realization. Perseus proceeds with divine help through various stages to his goal, and he approaches and decapitates Medusa as the archetypal monster-killer, reminding us of Marduk, St George, Beowulf and any number of 'saviours' who rid the world of monstrosities; these in turn represent the demon within, which must be confronted in our inner selves if we are to find a way to wholeness. Perseus finds such wholeness on his return when he saves and marries Andromeda and rescues his mother. In relationship with these two non-monstrous females, he can achieve his proper place in the 'normal' world – and by extension, ours. It is important that during his heroic return from the dark world of the Gorgons, he overcomes resistance from the Titan Atlas and the evil king Polydektes by effectively turning the evil eye that is the head of Medusa into the Gorgoneion, which serves as a protective talisman.

As for Medusa, she is the very monster the hero needs; she is, in fact, the reason for his being. Without her he has nothing to do. In travelling to the ends of the earth in search of his goal, Perseus resembles heroes of many cultures who descend to the depths of existence to confront death and ultimate chaos. The archetypal essence of the Perseus-Medusa myth is centred in a hero's descent to an Underworld in order to destroy a universal human enemy. There are many myths from various traditions that give form to this archetype. In the Christian tradition Jesus, during his three days of death, descends to Hell to release fallen humanity. In India the beautiful Savitri, the daughter of the sun god and the embodiment of the Vedas, confronts Yama, the Vedic god of the dead, in the Underworld, and harnesses his knowledge of Brahman, the Logos or essence of creation. Herakles descends to overcome the three-headed, serpent-tailed monster dog Cerberus, the hound of death and hell.

A story that strikes a strangely similar archetypal chord to that of the story of Perseus and Medusa is the myth of the descent of Inanna-Ishtar, the Sumerian-Baylonian goddess of fertility and life. Inanna feels driven to know the reality of her sister Ereshkigal – her monstrous opposite. Only by confronting her sister can she understand death and thus return to the world above with the power of that knowledge, power that, combined with her own already existing power, will allow her to fulfil her role as Queen of the Above. Inanna goes to her Underworld sister because that is the only way she can become a whole being. Perseus makes the seemingly foolish announcement that he will kill Medusa, because he needs Medusa's power in order to be the whole Perseus.

This is the night journey of the soul. The heroes descend to the Underworld to obtain something that will benefit the upper world. Perseus decapitates Medusa with an agricultural instrument, a sickle. Perseus' descent, like all such heroic descents, is an attempt to bring the light of consciousness and reason into the depths of the unconscious and in so doing to *harvest* the powers of the Other. The 'stupefying look' is conquered. The Medusa head becomes a talisman, a universal Gorgoneion which Perseus uses to destroy his enemies. Athene places it on her shield.

Athene is a central figure here. We remember that Palaephatus tells us that Athene was referred to by the Cernaeans as 'Gorgon'. In a sense this appellation is apt. Just as Inanna is one side of a being whose opposite is Erishkigal, Athene is united to Medusa. But their being female – so important in the purely Greek cultural context – is secondary to a general psychological connection. Athene 'hates' Medusa because she is the dark side of her being – the other side of the mirror. Athene is wisdom, reason and order; Medusa is the entropic chaos that threatens wisdom, reason and order. Athene is Perseus' alter ego, his conscience, the positive side of his unconscious being, in Jungian terms his anima. As such, she guides his hand in the decapitation of Medusa, her shadow, the dark side of the unconscious, the demon within. In the descent to Medusa for the ritual sacrifice, Athene needs the hero figure – the monster-slayer – because the monster-slayer is us, our collective ego, which must make sense of the conflicting forces within. If Athene committed the act herself it would mean nothing to us.

It is when the myth is approached as a version of a universal collective dream that Perseus' true significance is revealed. Modern commentators have concentrated on Medusa when they approach this myth, almost sometimes to the exclusion of Perseus. Yet without Perseus, Medusa is little more than a nasty monster living harmlessly at the edge of existence. Medusa, as Jane Harrison and others have pointed out, was first and foremost a head separated from an ancient body by Perseus. By decapitating Medusa and bringing back her head, Perseus provides his culture with the power to overcome the evil eye, the petrifying stare and the ancient earth-based mysteries. He provides the Gorgoneion and makes possible the social order and 'normal' relationships, represented by his marriage with the beautiful but pliant Andromeda.

Without Perseus, Medusa is just one of many archaic monsters of the Gaian period. With Perseus she comes into her own, becomes meaningful to us, too – becomes a part of our psychic life. It is Perseus who, in effect, releases her power to fascinate us. It is Perseus with whom we identify as he pursues his goal. We can relate his quest – its beginning, middle and end, its plot – to our own passage through life or through a psychological growth process. To relate to Medusa we need Perseus. Medusa is merely the immediate goal of Perseus' quest. Perseus' life is our life, his quest our quest. Like him or not, we are on his side, not Medusa's, unless we cloak the Gorgon in an ideology or belief system that masks rather than reveals her. The heroes born in world mythology are all different, all cultural phenomena, just as all of us are born as particular familial and cultural expressions. But, like the heroes who represent us, we all share the human awareness of a path. Of the species of our planet, as far as we know, we alone are aware of plot, of the past and the future in relation to the present, of beginnings, middles and ends. We are obsessed with where we came from and where we will go. What defines us as a species is our sense of a linear road of life. Medusa always lurks on that road. Like all inner demons, she is protected by various defence mechanisms that the dream persona must overcome. The Graiae, her monstrous sisters – limited to one tooth and one eye – are the absurd methods we use to deny our Medusas. Her fellow Gorgon sisters are more serious sources of denial. Once the dream persona gets by these gatekeepers, the tools needed to face the monster – the hat, the *kibisis*, the winged sandals – become available. And then Medusa is there before us. Whether she takes the form of a femme fatale, a beautiful victim, a fear of castration, an intellectual symbol of the Other or a punk goth, she is the demonic self that can cause the stony immobility of narcissism. With knowledge of the demon's power and the clear mirror of consciousness, the self avoids the look of the monster and, with the help of the tools procured and wisdom's sword, separates the demonic gaze from its body and brings it into the light of consciousness. The creative energy and power once imprisoned in the demon can now serve the dreamer who, like the freed winged horse Pegasus, can spring with bright abandon from the severed body of the monster within.

But the story does not end there. Perseus returns home with his Medusa head and finds his Andromeda. In terms of the overall collective dream, it might be said that Medusa has gradually come back to life in her pre-demonic form. The dreamer is all the characters in a dream. So it is that we are Medusa, Perseus and Andromeda. Imprisoned as the Other at the fringes of existence, Medusa was a petrifying monster. Freed from that state by the dreamer's sword, she can emerge from the Underworld transformed as Andromeda. The union of Perseus and Andromeda symbolizes the psychic wholeness that is the ultimate goal of the Medusa dream.

BIBLIOGRAPHY

Adler, Amy, 'Performance Anxiety: Medusa, Sex, and the First Amendment', *Yale Journal of Law and the Humanities*, 227 (Summer 2009); originally 'Medusa: A Glimpse of the Woman in First Amendment Law' (working paper)

Aikin, John, and Anna Laetitia Barbould, 'An Enquiry into Those Kinds of Distress which Excite Agreeable Sensations . . .', in *Miscellaneous Pieces in Prose* (London, 1773)

Albrecht, Thomas, *The Medusa Effect: Representations and Epistemology in Victorian Aesthetics* (Albany, NY, 2009)

Alighieri, Dante, *Inferno*, Canto 9, in *The Divine Comedy of Dante Alighieri*, trans. Allan Mandelbaum (Berkeley and Los Angeles, CA, 1980)

Apollodorus, *Library (Biblioteca)*, Book 2, trans. James George Frazer (Cambridge, MA, 1990)

Apollonius Rhodius, *Argonautica*, trans. R. C. Seaton (Cambridge, MA, 1988), 397 (IV, 1512–1517)

Arnulf of Orleans, *Aurelianensis Glosule super Lucanum*, ed. Berthe M. Marti, in *Papers and Monographs of the American Academy of Rome* (Rome, 1958)

—, [Commentary on Ovid] 'Un cultore di Ovidio nel secolo XII', *Memorie del R. Istituto Lombardo di Scienze e Lettere*, XXIV/4 (Milan, 1932)

Augustine of Hippo, *De Civitate Dei* (City of God), trans. Henry Bettenson (Harmondsworth, 1972)

—, *Confessions*, trans. A. C. Outler (Philadelphia, PA, 1955)

Bacon, Francis, *The Wisdom of the Ancients* (Kila, MT, 1992)

Barnes, Hazel E., 'The Look of the Gorgon', in *Meddling Gods: Four Essays on Classical Themes* (Lincoln, NE, 1974)

Barth, John, *Chimera* (New York, 1972)

Barthes, Roland, 'Méduse-Medusa', in *Roland Barthes*, trans. Richard

Howard (New York, 1977)
Benjamin, Walter, 'Paris, Capital of the Nineteenth Century', in *The Arcades Project*, trans. Howard Eiland and Kevin McLaughlin (Cambridge, MA, 1999)
Berger, Maurice, 'Edward Burne-Jones' "Perseus Cycle" and the Vulnerable Medusa', *Arts Magazine*, LIV/8 (1980), pp. 149–53
Boccaccio, Giovanni, *Genealogy of the Pagan Gods*, trans. Jon Solomon (Cambridge, MA, 2011)
Boer, C., ed., '*Ovide moralisé*': *Poèm du commencement du quatorzième siècle*, 5 vols (Amsterdam, 1915–38)
Bowers, Susan, 'Medusa and the Female Gaze', *NWSA Journal*, II/2 (1990), pp. 217–35
Caillois, Roger, *The Mask of Medusa*, trans. George Ordish (New York, 1964)
Campbell, Joseph, *The Hero With a Thousand Faces* (Princeton, NJ, 1972)
—, *The Masks of God*, 4 vols (New York, 1970)
Carballido, Emilio, *Medusa* (Englewood Cliff, NJ, 1972)
Cixous, Hélène, 'The Laugh of the Medusa', trans. Kieth Cohen and Paula Cohen, *Signs*, I/4 (Summer 1976)
Collins, William, 'Ode to Fear', in *The Poetical Works of William Collins* (Boston, MA, 1865)
Conti, Natale, *Natale Conti's Mythologies: A Select Translation*, trans. Anthony DiMatteo (New York, 1994)
Culpepper, Emily Erwin, 'Ancient Gorgons: A Face for Contemporary Women's Rage', *Woman of Power: A Magazine of Feminism, Spirituality and Politics,* 3 (Winter/Spring 1986)
Currie, Charlotte, 'Transforming Medusa', *Amaltea: Revista de Mitocrítica*, 3 (2011), pp. 169–81
De Lauretis, Teresa, *Alice Doesn't: Feminism, Semiotics, Cinema* (Bloomington, IN, 1984)
Derrida, Jacques, *Glas*, trans. John P. Leavy Jr and Richard Rand (Lincoln, NE, 1986)
Diodorus Siculus, *The Historical Library*, trans. G. Booth (Ann Arbor, MI, 2006), Book 3
Doty, William C., *The Study of Myths and Rituals* (Tuscaloosa, AL, 1986)
Douglas, N., 'Dragons', *English Review*, 16 (1914), pp. 562–8
Drake, Nathan, 'On Objects of Terror', in *Literary Hours* (London, 1800)
Dumoulié, Camille, 'On Medusa', in *Companion to Literary Myths*, ed. Pierre Brunel, trans. Wendy Allatson (London and New York, 1992)
Durrell, Lawrence, 'Corfu', in *The Greek Islands* (New York, 1978)
Ebreo, Leone (Abravanel), *The Philosophy of Love*, trans. F. Friedeberg-Seeley and Jean H. Barnes (London, 1937)

Eliade, Mircea, *Myth and Reality* (New York, 1963)
—, *The Myth of the Eternal Return* (Princeton, NJ, 1965)
—, *Patterns in Comparative Religion* (Cleveland, OH, 1963)
Euripides, *Ion*, trans. Gilbert Murray (London, 1954)
Evans, Jonathan D., 'The Dragon', in *Mythical and Fabulous Creatures: A Source Book and Research Guide*, ed. Malcolm South (New York and Westport, CT, 1987), pp. 27–58
Ferenczi, Sándor, 'On the Symbolism of the Head of Medusa', in *Further Contributions to the Theory and Technique of Psycho-analysis*, trans. Jane Isabel Suttie et al., ed. John Rickman (London, 1962)
Franz, Marie-Louise von, *Shadow and Evil in Fairy Tales* (Boston, MA, and London, 1995)
Frazer, Sir James George, *The New Golden Bough*, ed. Theodor Gaster (New York, 1964)
Frecerro, John, 'Medusa: The Letter and the Spirit', *Yearbook of Italian Studies* (1972)
Freud, Sigmund, 'Medusa's Head' and 'The Infantile Genital Organization', in *The Standard Edition of the Complete Psychological Works of Sigmund Freud,* ed. and trans. James Strachey (New York, 1999)
Frontisi-Ducroux, Françoise, 'La Gorgone: Paradigme de création d'images', *Les Cahiers du College Iconique: Communications et Débats*, I (1993). Partially reprinted as 'The Gorgon Paradigm of Image Creation', trans. Seth Graebner (1999), in *The Medusa Reader*, ed. Marjorie Garber and Nancy J. Vickers (New York and London, 2003), pp. 262–7
Fulgentius, *Mythologies*, trans. Leslie George Whitbread (Columbus, OH, 1971)
Garber, Marjorie, 'MacBeth: The Male Medusa', in *Shakespeare's Ghost Writers: Literature as Uncanny Causality* (New York, 1987)
Garber, Marjorie, and Nancy J. Vickers, eds, *The Medusa Reader* (New York and London, 2003)
Gaster, Theodor, *The Oldest Stories in the World* (Boston, MA, 1952)
Gimbutas, Marija A., *The Goddesses and Gods of Old Europe, 6500–3500 BC: Myths and Cult Images* (London, 1982)
Goethe, Johann Wolfgang von, 'Comments on the Rondanini Medusa', in Lizbeth Goodman, 'Who's Looking at Who(m)?: Reviewing Medusa', *Modern Drama*, XXXIX/I (Spring 1996)
Goodman, Lizbeth, 'Who's Looking at Who(m): Re-viewing Medusa', *Modern Drama*, XXXIX/I (Spring 1996), pp. 190–210
Graves, Robert, *The Greek Myths*, 2 vols (Baltimore, MD, 1955), esp. I:127, 129, 174–5, 237–45
—, *The White Goddess: A Historical Grammar of Poetic Myth*, revd edn (New York, 1966)

Harrington, John, Preface to Ariosto's *Orlando Furioso*, trans. John Harrington (Oxford, 1972)

Harris, Bud, and Masimilla M. Harris, 'Facing the Death Mother: A Guide for Healing our Feminine Selves and Moving from Paralysis to Full Vitality and Creativity' (28 October 2011), audio CD, www.budharris.com

Harrison, Jane Ellen, *Prolegomena to the Study of Greek Religion* (Princeton, NJ, 1991)

Heath, Stephen, 'Difference', *Screen*, XIX/3 (1978)

Hertz, Neil, 'Medusa's Head: Male Hysteria under Political Pressure', *Representations*, 4 (Fall 1983)

Hesiod, *The Works and Days; Theogony; The Shield of Herakles*, trans. Richard Lattimore (Ann Arbor, MI, 1991)

Hiebert, Ted, 'The Medusa Complex: A Theory of Stoned Posthumanism', *Drain Journal of Arts and Culture*, 5 (Fall 2005)

Hillman, James, *The Myth of Analysis: Three Essays in Archetypal Psychology* (Evanston, IL, 1983/9)

Homer, *Iliad*, trans. Richard Lattimore (Chicago, IL, 1961), Books V and XI

—, *Odyssey*, trans. Robert Fitzgerald (New York, 1998), Book XI: 635

Hopkins, Clark, 'Assyrian Elements in the Perseus-Gorgon Story', *American Journal of Archeology*, XXXVIII/3 (July–September 1934), pp. 341–58

Huot, Sylvia, 'The Medusa Interpolation in the *Roman de la rose*: Mythographic Program and Ovidian Intertext', *Speculum*, LXIV/4 (October 1987), pp. 865–77

Jacobs, Carol, 'On Looking at Shelley's Medusa', *The Lesson of Paul de Man*, Yale French Studies 69, (1985), pp. 163–79

Jung, Carl Gustav, *The Archetypes of the Collective Unconscious* (Princeton, NJ, 1959)

—, *Symbols of Transformation* (Princeton, NJ, 1976)

—, and Carl Kerenyi, *Essays on a Science of Mythology: The Myth of the Divine Child and the Mysteries of Eleusis* (Princeton, NJ, 1969)

Keats, John, 'La Belle Dame Sans Merci', in *The Complete Poems of John Keats* (New York, 1994)

Klindienst, Patricia, 'The Voice of the Shuttle is Ours', *Stanford Literature Review*, I/I (Spring 1984), pp. 25–33

Knight, Richard Payne, *The Symbolical Language of Ancient Art and Mythology* (New York, 1877)

Kofman, Sarah, *The Enigma of Woman: Woman in Freud's Writing*, trans. Catherine Porter (Ithaca, NY, 1985)

Koslow, Susan, 'The Science and Poetics of *The Head of Medusa* by Rubens and Snyders', *Shop Talk: Studies in Honor of Seymour Slive*

(Cambridge, MA, 1995), pp. 147–9
Leeming, David A., *Myth: A Biography of Belief* (Oxford and New York, 2002)
—, 'The Chimera', in *Mythical and Fabulous Creatures: A Source Book and Research Guide*, ed. Malcolm South (New York and Westport, CT, 1987), pp. 103–12
—, *The Oxford Companion to World Mythology* (Oxford and New York, 2005)
—, *The World of Myth* (Oxford and New York, 1990)
—, and Jake Page, *Goddess: Myths of the Female Divine* (Oxford and New York, 1994)
London, Jack, *The Mutiny of Elsinore* (Honolulu, HI, 1987)
Lorris, Guillaume de, and Jean de Meun, *The Romance of the Rose*, trans. Frances Horgan (New York and Oxford, 1999)
Lucan, *Pharsalia*, trans. Robert Graves (Baltimore, MA, 1957)
Lucian, *The Hall*, trans. A. M. Harmon, vol. I (Cambridge, MA, 1961)
McElroy, Colleen J., 'A Navy Blue Afro', in *Music from Home: Selected Poems* (Carbondale, IL, 1975)
McGann, Jerome J., 'The Beauty of the Medusa', *Studies in Romanticism* (Winter 1971), pp. 3–25
Marin, Louis, *To Destroy Painting*, trans. Mette Hjort (Chicago, IL, 1995)
Martill, David M., 'Medusa Effect: Instantaneous Fossilization', *Geology Today* (November–December 1989), pp. 201–5
Marx, Karl, *Capital*, trans. Samuel Moore and Edward Aveling, in *The Marx-Engels Reader*, ed. Robert C. Tucker (New York, 1978)
Milton, John, *The Poetic Works of John Milton*, ed. William Aldis Wright (Cambridge and New York, 2011)
Neumann, Eric, *The Great Mother: An Analysis of the Archetype*, trans. R.F.C. Hull (Princeton, NJ, 1963)
—, *The Origins and History of Consciousness*, trans R.F.C. Hull (Princeton, NJ, 1982)
Nietzsche, Friedrich, *The Birth of Tragedy*, in *The Basic Writings of Nietzsche* (New York, 1968)
Ovid, *Ovid's Metamorphoses*, trans. Charles Boer (Dallas, TX, 1989), Books IV and V
Palaephatus, *On Unbelievable Tales*, trans. Jacob Stern (Wauconda, IL, 1996)
Pater, Walter, 'Leonardo da Vinci', in *Walter Pater: Three Major Texts*, ed. William E. Buckler (New York, 1986), pp. 134–52
Patterson, Kent, 'A Terrible Beauty: Medusa in Three Victorian Poets', *Tennessee Studies in Literature*, 17 (1972), pp. 111–20
Pausanias, *Description of Greece*, trans. W.H.S. Jones, vol. I (Cambridge, MA, 1933)

Pautrat, Bernard, 'Nietzsche Medused', in *Looking After Nietzsche*, ed. Laurence A. Rickles, trans. Peter Connor (Albany, NY, 1990), pp. 159–73
Petrarch, *Petrarch's Lyric Poems: The 'Rime sparse' and Other Lyrics*, trans. Robert M. Durling (Cambridge, MA, 1979)
Pindar, twelfth Pythian ode, in *Odes of Pindar*, trans. Geoffrey S. Conway (London, 1972)
Pizan, Christine de, *The Book of the City of Ladies*, trans. Earl Jeffrey Richards (New York, 1982)
Plath, Sylvia, *The Collected Poems*, ed. Ted Hughes (New York, 1981)
Potts, Albert M., 'The Eye of Medusa', in *The World's Eye* (Lexington, KY, 1982)
Praz, Mario, 'The Beauty of the Medusa', in *The Romantic Agony* (New York, 1978)
Richards, Justin, *The Medusa Effect* (London, 1998)
Rogers, Neville, 'Shelley and the Visual Arts', *Keats-Shelley Memorial Bulletin*, 12 (1961)
Roman de la rose, ed. Ernest Langlois (Paris, 1924)
Rossetti, Dante Gabriel, 'Aspecta Medusa', in *Collected Works of Dante Gabriel Rossetti*, vol. I (London, 1987)
Sarton, May, 'The Muse as Medusa', in *Collected Poems (1930–1973)* (New York, 1974)
Sartre, Jean-Paul, *Being and Nothingness: A Phenomenological Essay on Ontology*, trans. Hazel E. Barnes (London, 2000)
Scott, Grant F., 'Shelley, Medusa, and the Perils of Ekphrasis', in *The Romantic Imagination: Literature and Art in England and Germany*, ed. Frederick Burwick and Jürgen Klein, Studies in Comparative Literature 6 (Amsterdam and Atlanta, GA, 1996), pp. 315–32
Seal, Mark, 'The Versace Moment', *American Way*, XXIX/15 (August 1996)
Shelley, Percy Bysshe, 'On the Medusa of Leonardo da Vinci in the Florentine Gallery', in *The Complete Poetical Works of Percy Bysshe Shelley* (London, 1934)
Siebers, Tobin, *The Mirror of Medusa* (Christchurch, NZ, 2000)
Silvestris, Bernadus, *Commentary on the First Six Books of Virgil's Aeneid*, trans. Earl G. Schreiber and Thomas E. Maresca (Lincoln, NE, 1979)
Slater, Philip, *The Glory of Hera: Greek Mythology and the Greek Family* (Boston, MA, 1968), pp. 308–36
Smartt, Dorothea, 'Medusa', in *Mythic Women/Real Women: Plays and Performance Pieces by Women*, ed. Lizbeth Goodman (London, 2000), pp. 259–62

Spenser, Edmund, *The Faerie Queene*, ed. Thomas Roche and C. Patrick O'Donnell (London and New York, 1979)
Stanford, Ann, 'Medusa', in *In Mediterranean Air* (New York, 1977)
South, Malcolm, ed., *Mythical and Fabulous Creatures: A Source Book and Research Guide* (New York and Westport, CT, 1987)
Suther, Judith D., 'The Gorgon Medusa', in *Mythical and Fabulous Creatures: A Source Book and Research Guide*, ed. Malcolm South (New York and Westport, CT, 1987), pp. 163–78
Tertullian, *De cultu feminarum*, 1:1, Part 2, in *The Ante-Nicene Christian Library: Translations of the Fathers down to AD 325*, ed. Alexander Roberts and James Donaldson, 24 vols (Edinburgh, 1866–72), vol. IV
Theweleit, Klaus, *Male Fantasies* (Minneapolis, MN, 1987)
Vasari, Giorgio, *Lives of the Artists*, trans. George Bull (New York, 1965), pp. 258–60
Vernant, Jean-Pierre, *Mortals and Immortals*, trans. Thomas Curley and Froma I. Zeitlin (Princeton, NJ, 1991)
Walker, Barbara G., *The Woman's Encyclopedia of Myths and Secrets* (San Francisco, 1983)
Walker, Julia M., *Medusa's Mirrors: Spenser, Shakespeare, Milton and the Metamorphosis of the Feminine Self* (Cranbury, NJ, 1998)
Webster, T.B.L., *From Mycenae to Homer* (New York, 1958)
Wiese, Robert, 'Variant Medusas: Creative Incarnations' (24 March 2006), at www.wizards.com
Wilk, Stephen R., *Medusa: Solving the Mystery of the Gorgon* (Oxford and New York, 2000)

ACKNOWLEDGEMENTS

I wish to thank Ben Hayes at Reaktion Books for suggesting this project and for supporting me with good ideas throughout its production. Any biography – perhaps especially one of a mythological subject – is dependent on earlier explorations. I am particularly indebted to the good and comprehensive collection of Medusa materials in *The Medusa Reader*, edited by Marjorie Garber and Nancy J. Vickers (New York and London, 2003) and to Professor Dalia Kandiyoti at the City University of New York for her suggestions about the feminist approach to Medusa.

'Medusa of the Snakes' © Ann Forfreedom, from *Book of the Goddess*, ed. Ann Forfreedom and Julie Ann (Temple of the Goddess Within, 1980).

'A Navy Blue Afro' © Colleen J. McElroy, reprinted with permission.

The author and publishers wish to express their thanks to the below sources of illustrative material and/or permission to reproduce it. (Some locations uncredited in the captions for reasons of brevity are also given below.)

British Museum, London (photos © The Trustees of the British Museum): pp. 24 (top), 25, 27, 28; Cleveland Museum of Art, Cleveland, Ohio: p. 24 (foot); Galleria degli Uffizi, Florence: p. 47; Glyptothek, Munich: p. 45; Heraklion Archaeological Museum, Crete: p. 89; Kunsthistorisches Museum, Vienna: p. 41; Loggia della Signoria, Florence: p. 95; Magdalene College, Oxford: p. 21; Musée du Louvre, Paris: p. 54; Museo Archeologico Regionale Paolo Orsi, Syracuse, Sicily: pp. 22, 23; Musei Vaticani, Vatican City: p. 46; private collections: pp. 42, 53, 56; Staatsgalerie Stuttgart: p. 52; State Hermitage Museum, St Petersburg: p. 11.

INDEX